SHAPING COLLEGE WRITING

PARAGRAPH AND ESSAY

Joseph D. Gallo
Henry W. Rink

FOOTHILL COLLEGE

HARCOURT, BRACE & WORLD, INC.

NEW YORK | CHICAGO | SAN FRANCISCO | ATLANTA

ISBN: 0-15-580857-5

Library of Congress Catalog Card Number: 68-22215

Printed in the United States of America

Preface

As a beginning exercise in composition, paragraph-writing recommends itself on several counts. The paragraph is the smallest prose unit that lends itself to a close analysis of unity, coherence, and systematic arrangement of thought. If well constructed, it resembles the complete theme in its support of a central idea by means of specifics. Ideally, it is long enough to demand some continuity of thought yet, at the same time, short enough for the student to grasp as a whole. At its best, it represents an essay in miniature.

As such, the paragraph seems to us to be the best medium for introducing the student to pattern, structure, and arrangement in prose writing without immediately overwhelming him with the complexities of the full-length essay. The beginning student is too often asked to learn at least twenty new skills at once and, what is more, to perform them all competently. Of course, practicing paragraph-writing does not guarantee every student success in all writing skills, but it helps him master the fundamentals of good writing. Teaching the student to make the eventual transition from the paragraph to the essay seems to us more logical than starting with the whole and then, only as a kind of afterthought, considering its parts.

Once the student has developed a firm sense of the structure that underlies a well-organized paragraph, he is ready—we believe—to make the transition to the multi-paragraph paper. He will have gradually acquired the confidence that comes from learning to impose order on his thoughts. He has discovered that his ideas can be arranged systematically, that there are means of imposing coherence upon diverse materials. Perhaps, as he finds the paragraph increasingly confining, he is also discovering that there is more in the world to write about than he had imagined and that he can exert some measure of control over what he finally does choose to treat. Most importantly, he sees that the difference between a well-structured paragraph and a unified essay is one of size rather than of kind.

The movement from the most basic unit of paragraph-writing to the construction of the whole paragraph is reflected in the order of the chapters in *Shaping College Writing: Paragraph and Essay*. The first chapter stresses the topic sentence with its important controlling idea that helps the student focus his thoughts and organize his writing around the main idea of the paragraph. Chapters 2 and 3 deal with unity and coherence. Chapter 4 discusses specific sources of support and stresses the student's responsibility to check and document the material he uses. Chapter 5 directs the student's attention to the organization of the whole paragraph and introduces the similarities between the paragraph and the essay. In Chapter 6, the student sees the contents of the one-paragraph paper expressed in diagrams that show the rhetorical relationships of its beginning, middle, and end.

Chapter 7 allows the student and teacher to extend the principles of organization and form of a one-paragraph paper to a multi-paragraph paper. What we stress in the generalizations governing this extension is that the relationships are the same and that the difference is one of scale. A five-paragraph paper is used as the archetype of longer essays, and the student is offered what we hope will be a guide in future writing: the *one-three-nine* structure.

Since this book does not pretend to be a grammar or a reader or a manual on usage, we recommend the use of any supplementary textbooks that the teacher believes are suitable for his course. We feel our book is adaptable to any basic composition course in which emphasis is placed on the principles of structure and concrete support as means of instructing the student to write. To this end exercises have been devised, not to offer the student instant formulas for writing but rather to help him see structural elements that characterize most well-written prose.

We extend our gratitude to all our colleagues who helped us, joked with us, and encouraged us. Our special thanks must go to Mrs. Vernon S. Appleby of DeAnza College, who class-tested all the exercises and gave us invaluable suggestions for revision. But perhaps our greatest debt is to our students at Foothill College, who, over the past five years, have helped us discover what sorts of pedagogical techniques will work in teaching composition.

Joseph D. Gallo

Henry W. Rink

Contents

1 The Topic Sentence

The dominating idea of any paragraph is contained in a key sentence known as the *topic sentence*. This topic sentence—most often found at the beginning of a paragraph—contains the kernel or essence of the subject the paragraph deals with. It is, of course, the most important sentence in the paragraph, and it is in the form of a generalization, which is supported or proved by specific facts in the remaining sentences of that paragraph. It may be helpful at this point to examine the difference between a generalization and a specific statement:

A Generalization	B Specific Statement
Most coeds wish to be seen wearing popular clothing styles.	Marnie Ellison, a tiny blonde, wore a plaid miniskirt and white woolen stockings.
Freshmen often find the first week of college confusing.	Fifteen minutes after the bell, a gangling, dark-haired boy who looked athletic was wandering about in the rain asking everyone he met the way to L-26.

A session in Dr. Malcolm's economics class is a boring experience.	In a voice as soothing as a lullaby, Professor Malcolm reads large chunks of factual information from the old black binder that houses his undergraduate notes.

It is important that the student recognize immediately the difference between the generalization and the specific statement. Note that in column **A** of the examples, the sentences are of a broad, nonspecific nature. They resemble the sorts of sweeping statements we make about the world around us: "Most people are basically dishonest"; or "It usually rains at the beach during spring vacation"; or even an old cliché like "He who laughs last laughs best." The statements in column **B**, on the other hand, are focused upon specific objects or events. Each could be used as a single example in support of its companion sentence in column **A**. The specific statements are more concrete — that is, they make reference to individuals (*Marnie Ellison*), colors (*plaid, white*), places (*L-26*), time (*fifteen minutes*), articles of clothing (*woolen stockings*), unique physical characteristics (*gangling, dark-haired, tiny*), and weather conditions (*rain*).

Hereafter in this book, generalizations will be used mostly as topic sentences. But to support or develop those generalizations, specific statements will be required. Specifics are the substance of writing, and, to put it bluntly, in the intellectual world a person may not support a generalization by means of other generalizations. One looks silly trying to convince thoughtful people that he knows what he's talking about when all he has to offer are vague generalities. For proof of this statement we might glance at a student paragraph that begins with the topic sentence about Dr. Malcolm:

> A session in Dr. Malcolm's economics class is a boring experience. Dr. Malcolm does not know how to liven up a class. He's afraid to do anything exciting or startling. His classes are monotonous and boring for the student. He probably knows a lot about his subject, but his presentation of it leaves much to be desired. His students never get interested in the subject of economics, which should be a pretty great thing to study. As a result, Dr. Malcolm is not a very popular college instructor.

Notice that any one of the sentences in this paragraph could probably be substituted for the topic sentence. Each sentence is a generalization used by the writer to try to support the main idea of the paragraph, and, as a result, the reader is left wondering what specifically causes Dr. Malcolm's class to be so uninspiring. What do we really know about him after reading the paragraph? Does the man periodically doze at the lectern? Does he turn his back on the class? Has he a speech defect? Is he so bitingly sarcastic toward the class that he tends to become tiresome, as most sarcastic people do? Or is he simply a harmless drudge? Such a topic sentence as the one above usually causes the reader to ask the question *Why?* It is his right to have that question answered by facts, and it is the writer's obligation to answer the question by providing those facts. In the above paragraph, of course, the student is playing that old game called "putting the teacher on."

Such an approach to college writing is doomed to failure, because the writer does not produce facts that will convincingly support his topic sentence. Obviously, to be respected in the intellectual world one must be able to bring factual information to the defense of his ideas. So don't be tempted to take the easy way out and hand in a paragraph that is only a string of generalizations.

The Controlling Idea

Most workable topic sentences may be thought of as having three distinct parts: subject, verb, and controlling idea. The *subject* is, of course, what the sentence is all about; it indicates the general area to be dealt with. The *verb* makes a statement about the subject. The *controlling idea* usually follows these main parts and describes or makes a judgment about the subject, as in the following example:

subj.   *verb*   *c. i.*

T. S.:   The poet D. M. Carlson has proved himself a [sensitive observer of nature].

In the above example you can easily see that the subject of the topic sentence is *the poet D. M. Carlson.* A unified paragraph on all the attributes, personal and professional, of anyone would run the length of a book. Therefore, the writer must select one aspect of Carlson's personality or career that the paragraph will develop. That vast subject is then narrowed in the part of the topic sentence that describes or makes a judgment about the subject — namely, by the controlling idea. The main function of the controlling idea, then, is to focus or narrow the subject. Thus, the student using the above example as his topic sentence would deal only with Carlson's sensitive observation of nature in his poetry. The writer could use examples from certain poems to illustrate this point. However, he must never begin talking about Carlson's private life, his popularity as a poet, his personal peculiarities, his love of fine cars, or the fistfights he's had. The controlling idea provides against such rambling.

The controlling idea may be conveniently viewed as a contract the writer makes with the reader — a kind of promise to talk only about the portion of the subject that is expressed in the controlling idea. True to its name, the controlling idea acts as a controller or limiter of what will be discussed in a paragraph. As soon as the writer's supporting sentences stray from the controlling idea, he has broken the contract he made with the reader.

A controlling idea can come in several forms. It may be a short phrase, as it is in the example about D. M. Carlson. It may be simply a descriptive word, often an adjective, which explains or limits the subject. Consider the following example:

T. S.:   One can hardly deny that Harley Klentz is a [sloppy dresser].

3

In this topic sentence, the controlling idea is made up of a noun and an adjective describing that noun. In a paragraph about Harley Klentz, the writer would develop the descriptive word *sloppy* as it applied to Klentz's various garments.

Often the controlling idea is a single descriptive word, as it is in the following sentence:

> T. S.: Most of his friends would agree that Brumley Sinkwich is [generous].

When the controlling idea is a descriptive word, such as it is in the above instance, it is helpful if you define it, especially if it isn't a commonly used term. Of course, we know what *generous* means, but if the term you choose happens to be *magnanimous* or *eccentric,* you may need to look it up in a dictionary to be sure of its meaning. After all, it would be embarrassing to find, upon checking the dictionary, that your paragraph had nothing to do with the actual meaning of the controlling idea.

Thus, it is of great importance that you recognize what your controlling idea is and that the controlling idea be readily limited and defined. It may also be helpful if you position that controlling idea toward the end of your topic sentence so that the idea is the last thing the reader sees before getting to the supporting information. The following examples may help you see how topic sentences that take in too large an area may be improved by the writer's restricting the controlling idea:

Rudimentary Topic Sentence	Revision
Cerebros College has a beautiful campus.	The landscaping at Cerebros makes symmetrical use of shade trees.

Obviously, a word such as *symmetrical* is much more readily defined than one such as *beautiful,* a term that both philosophers and English instructors have been haggling over for centuries. Notice also that in the revision the area under discussion is reduced from an entire campus — which couldn't be covered adequately even in a twenty-page essay, let alone a paragraph — to one attractive feature of that campus, the positioning and arrangement of the various shade trees. Let's try another example:

Rudimentary Topic Sentence	Revision
Cerebros College has many interesting features.	Visitors to Cerebros have described the architecture of a typical building as modified oriental.

Interesting is the sort of adjective one uses to describe a modern painting that he doesn't understand but is too embarrassed to criticize; it's a word that gets a person off the hook without committing himself. *Interesting* means about a thousand things, most of them vague. *Modified oriental,* on the other hand, gives us a mental picture of the building being described. Again, notice that we have decreased the scope of our description from *many interesting features* to the architectural style of a single typical building on campus. Doesn't it seem to you more sensible to describe a single specific object than countless unspecified ones? We think you will be happier with the results you get by supporting the revised topic sentence; we know your instructor will.

Consider in this light the following example:

Rudimentary Topic Sentence	Revision
The area by the Cerebros library is a really neat place.	During the warm months the quad fronting the Cerebros library is a showplace for coed clothing styles.

Neat is a word that elderly maidens use to describe a living room, heavy drinkers to denote the process of taking a quick shot of straight whiskey, and teenage girls to describe Bob Dylan or the Beatles. Any term that is that readily applied to so many situations should be rejected by the student who wishes to write with precision. The revision gets down to earth: that vague *area* becomes *quad;* the quad isn't simply *by* the library, it faces it. Now we know what the writer had in mind when he used the term *neat:* girls and what girls wear.

As you have perhaps noticed in all the above examples, the writer was able to improve his topic sentence, to make it more workable, by choosing his controlling idea with care and by positioning it near the end of his topic sentence. Now let's try to duplicate the actual process of creating and refining a topic sentence with its controlling idea. Suppose you happened to glance over toward your neighbor's house on Saturday morning in time to see a large van delivering an expensive-looking red carpet. Not more than an hour later another van pulls up to unload a clothes drier and several articles of living-room furniture. Then your neighbor's wife arrives from the shopping center, her four shopping bags bulging with packages. That afternoon your neighbor complains about the bills his wife has been running up lately, and you recall that your girl friend is also pretty free with *your* money. You and your neighbor come to the conclusion that women enjoy living the good life. The process of arriving at this conclusion is the way topic sentences (and opinions and arguments) are made.

Now suppose the student puts that raw inference down in the form of a topic sentence:

Women enjoy living a good life.

Many students would choose such a sentence, and, what is more, would try to support it. But most first attempts can probably be improved and refined. Several things about this sentence bear some attention. In the first place, the adjective *good* has countless applications, even in a small dictionary. Try counting them if you don't believe us. Then, the good life itself has been the subject of dispute among thinkers ever since Socrates sprang the term upon the befuddled Athenians almost twenty-four centuries ago; thus, chances are that the student won't resolve the problem in a paragraph. Yet according to the above topic sentence he has committed himself to such a task, for the topic sentence is a promise to the reader to deliver the facts, although facts in support of such a sweeping statement may be hard to come by.

Now, what does the writer really mean? Perhaps some work with his topic sentence would improve it. He has made an observation about one woman's expenditures and has then come to a generalization about most women. Yet the topic sentence that came off the top of his head had nothing to do specifically with women spending men's money. What the student probably wants is the term *expensive* or, better yet, *extravagant*. Let's try it:

> Women are financially extravagant.

This is better, but it's still too big. No matter how hard he tried, a man obviously couldn't cram all the evidence in support of this statement into one paragraph. After making a quick trip around his own city block, he could find so many instances of women spending money like water that he would doubtless have enough evidence to fill a book. But suppose he concentrated on the lady next door or perhaps on his own girl friend? He then could narrow the focus of his topic sentence and still get in a gentle dig against all the ladies:

> Like most women, my girl Linda is financially extravagant.

Notice that here the writer has focused upon one woman who will more or less represent all her sisters in extravagance. Now, of course, it remains for the writer to prove to the skeptical reader that Linda is really a spendthrift and that she represents, to this extent, women in general. The process of supporting the topic sentence through specific facts is taken up in Chapter 4. Here we are concerned mostly with the controlling idea of the topic sentence and with whether that controlling idea can be supported within a single, unified paragraph. If you can't devise a topic sentence with a clearly defined controlling idea, chances are you can't produce a successful paragraph. Few paragraphs survive a poor topic sentence. Let's look at some workable topic sentences with their controlling ideas (their descriptive parts) underlined and then defined:

1. For winning the "Man of the Year" title, Miniver Winlocke received several appropriate awards.
   appropriate suitable, fitting, proper, suited to the honor or situation.
2. The typical Vietcong guerrilla is an efficient ground fighter.
   efficient working well, competent, producing the desired effect or result with the minimum effort.

6

3. Professor Pontoon can always be counted on to deliver a <u>disorderly</u> lecture.
   disorderly   messy, riotous, untidy, unsystematic, unruly.
4. When the going is hard, Al Prufrock usually sets a <u>cowardly</u> example.
   cowardly   having or showing lack of courage, extreme timidity.

This list is hardly complete, but it gives the student an idea of the sort of topic sentence that has a chance of working in a well-controlled paragraph. Observe how each one points toward the facts that will be used to support it. In the first sentence, for instance, the reader will expect the writer to identify the awards by name and description. The writer of the second topic sentence will have to list precisely those traits and characteristics that make the guerrilla an effective soldier. In the instance of the third sentence, the reader will want to know exactly what ingredients go into the production of Pontoon's chaotic lecture. In other words, the topic sentence points to the kind of facts that will then be used in its own support. Notice also that the controlling idea is usually placed close to the end of the sentence. Strategically speaking, the controlling idea might well be the last thing the reader sees before he gets into the support itself.

One other characteristic of most good topic sentences might be noted – their *brevity*. It is probably a valuable rule of thumb for the student to keep his topic sentences short and economical. Of course, to write a long, sophisticated sentence isn't against any law: that would be a narrow-minded rule. But the chances of the student's becoming confused and supporting the least important part of the topic sentence are great when the statement is wordy and involved. Consider the following perfectly workable topic sentence:

> Although only fifteen years old and the youngest member of a generally youthful and brilliant graduating class, Melvin Balloon has already invented several labor-saving household devices.

The inexperienced writer, if he devises such a sentence at all, is likely to focus on the fact that Melvin is young or that his class is youthful or even that his class is brilliant. Perhaps all these considerations have their place in the paragraph. But the important point is that brilliant young Melvin has invented several labor-saving devices; that's the point that needs to be supported. That's also the point that could get lost in such a sentence. So if the writer simply can't resist the urge to create long topic sentences, he should at least remember to place the main idea in the main or independent clause. That's a friendly warning that could save the student a lot of trouble.

A much more dire warning might be delivered about topic sentences that are likely to be losers from the start. Avoid what is sometimes called the dead-end topic sentence, one that either lacks a controlling idea or else doesn't point in any direction at all, such as the following:

7

1. The library is filled with books.
2. This campus has a total of 1,107 classrooms.
3. In 1492 Columbus discovered the New World.
4. Ronald Reagan and Pat Brown opposed each other in the 1966 California gubernatorial election.

To create topic sentences like those above is, for the writer, no great stroke of fortune, because none of the above statements lends itself to unified paragraph structure. None of them points toward any concise group of facts that could support it. Each lacks a controlling idea and tends to be too factual to act as a supportable generalization.

The wild guess is another kind of topic sentence that is to be avoided by the writer. Notice the following:

1. When I graduate from college, it shouldn't take me more than five years to own two cars and to move into a good neighborhood.
2. Most of the students in this class will probably settle in this area after graduation.

You must admit that it would be difficult to find facts in support of these generalizations. No facts exist, of course, that will reveal precisely what will happen next year. Only an expert can make an educated guess about the future on the basis of present trends. Remember, you are a writer, not a fortune teller.

Finally, it is a good policy to avoid posing a question as a topic sentence:

1. What is the significance of today's dance trends?
2. How can one write a good paper?

How indeed? A student could ramble on and on about such subjects. Assert yourself in this course! Know what you're writing about. Don't be tentative or questioning when you have facts to support a statement. Make the topic sentence a statement, not a cry for help.

Summary: Topic Sentence and Controlling Idea

1. The topic sentence contains the dominating generalization that a paragraph will develop.
2. The topic sentence is the writer's promise to the reader to deliver factual support.
3. The topic sentence should be placed at the beginning of the paragraph. It is easier to hang a paragraph from a key idea than to lead up to that idea.
4. The controlling idea is the heart of the topic sentence – its most vital organ.
5. The controlling idea is a word or phrase that is readily defined and limited.
6. The controlling idea is best placed toward the end of the topic sentence.

7. Although a topic sentence may contain more than one clause (as this sentence does), it is best to keep the sentence relatively short and concise.
8. If the writer chooses a complex topic sentence, the controlling idea should appear in the main clause. (Clauses will be discussed at greater length in the next chapter.)
9. Avoid the dead-end topic sentence, which lacks a controlling idea and points in no direction whatsoever.
10. Avoid the question and the prediction as topic sentences.

Writing a good topic sentence takes time and practice. The writer must often discard several prospective sentences before narrowing his final product down to a workable unit. But the job is essential, well worth the effort involved. For while it wouldn't exactly be true to say that a good topic sentence unconditionally guarantees a successful paragraph, without one you might just as well file your notebook and take your girl to a drive-in movie to see James Bond.

EXERCISE 1: *In the blank to the left, mark G if the sentence is a generalization and S if it is a specific.*

_____ 1. Sigmund Freud is one of the greatest names in medical history.
_____ 2. *The Poorhouse Fair* is John Updike's first novel.
_____ 3. Mario Andretti is a successful race-car driver.
_____ 4. On Labor Day in 1963 Mario Andretti won seven midget races—three in the afternoon at Flemington, New Jersey, and four at night in Hatfield, Pennsylvania.
_____ 5. Most people grow faint at the sight of blood.
_____ 6. U.S. military participation in Vietnam has been severely criticized by many of the nation's best minds.
_____ 7. In the July 1967 issue of *Esquire,* critic Dwight MacDonald called the Vietnam war "... a senseless atrocity, the least excusable war in our history...."
_____ 8. There has been a tremendous amount of controversy following the Warren Commission Report on the Kennedy assassination.
_____ 9. The book *The Immense Journey* by Loren Eiseley contains thirteen essays dealing with "the mysteries of man and nature."
_____ 10. Movies are becoming more and more daring in their subject matter.

EXERCISE 2: *This exercise is aimed at making clear the distinction between a generalization and a specific. For each of the following generalizations, supply one specific fact that supports the generalization.*

1. This classroom contains equipment that provides for an effective learning situation.

_____

_____

_____

2. The person who sits in front of me (behind, alongside) is dressed from head to toe in conventional, collegiate clothing.

_____

_____

_____

3. The architecture of this school has several distinctive characteristics.

_____

_____

_____

4. The range of Negro leadership in the civil rights movement is from excellent to poor.

_____

_____

_____

5. The instructor in this class displays certain mannerisms that draw student attention to him (her).

_____

_____

_____

6. Jacqueline Kennedy continues to be one of the most attractive women of our time.

_____

_____

_____

7. Cassius Clay, alias Muhammad Ali, has created a controversial public image for himself.

_____

_____

_____

8. The registration procedure at this school definitely has its shortcomings.

_____

_____

_____

9. So far in this course, we have studied certain requirements for writing an effective piece of prose.

_____

_____

_____

10. Many of today's rock 'n' roll groups are pretty unconventional in their physical appearance.

_____

_____

_____

EXERCISE 3: *In each of the following topic sentences, underline the word or phrase that represents the controlling idea of the sentence. Remember, the controlling idea is the narrowed-down part of the subject that will later be developed in the paragraph.*

1. In an August raid on Bass Landing, California, two gangs of motorcycle riders left the town a shambles.
2. Each day, Defense Secretary Clark Clifford accepts what to most men would be a staggering set of responsibilities.
3. At Green Bay, Paul Hornung was for years the National Football League's most versatile backfield man.
4. In London, Truman Capote's controversial book *In Cold Blood* recently got some inhospitable criticism from reviewer Kenneth Tynan.
5. Although they are scarcely observable on most maps, several islands off the coast of Baja California yield some of the world's richest sports fishing.

6. The late General Douglas MacArthur has been characterized, even by his friends, as a man with a healthy ego.
7. While it does have a certain romantic appeal, crop-dusting is not without its hazards.
8. Many college students today claim that their parents have unexciting forms of recreation.
9. Dr. Timothy Leary, founder of the League for Spiritual Discovery, has formulated a series of steps for achieving happiness.
10. In a vigorous sermon on the quality of most television programs, our pastor exclaimed against what he called "last season's tasteless series of shows."

EXERCISE 4:   *Many of the following topic sentences are either dead end or lacking in direction. Choose the one from each group that seems best adapted to the development of a paragraph. Look for a sentence that narrows down to a workable idea. Underline that idea.*

1. a. Classical composers are generally in a dream world of their own.
   b. Events in the short life of composer and pianist Frédéric Chopin reflect a great dedication to music.
   c. Chopin, who lived in France, was a great composer and pianist of the nineteenth century.
2. a. Suzanne Grimes was chosen last year's Miss America.
   b. The Miss America Pageant will always be one of America's favorite spectacles.
   c. The officials at the Miss America Pageant base their decisions on judgeable characteristics other than beauty alone.
3. a. The Warren Commission findings on the death of John F. Kennedy were published in 1965.
   b. The Warren Commission findings startled the nation.
   c. The single-assassin hypothesis of the Warren Commission has recently come under critical attack from a small group of writers.
4. a. For the Dodgers' Willie Davis, the second day of the 1966 World Series was a disaster.
   b. The Dodgers will always remember the '66 Series with red faces.
   c. Athletes have their ups and downs.
5. a. Tonight on Bruin turf two of the bitterest rivals in the Tri-County League will clash.
   b. Certain writers favor the Seahawks over the Bruins tonight.
   c. On the basis of season statistics, the Bruins are the pregame favorites over the Seahawks.
6. a. In a Mission District hotel last night, a tiny woman gave metropolitan police their fiercest battle of the year.
   b. A 24-year-old, 72-pound, 4-foot 4-inch woman was apprehended by police last night.

   c. A small, disreputable hotel in the Mission District was the scene of a hassle.

7. a. Science discovers some wonderful things.
   b. Doctors have recently discovered a new method to cut one's sleeping time in half.
   c. If used for too long, a recently discovered scientific method of cutting one's sleeping time produces distinct psychological changes in a person.

8. a. There have been countless Nobel Prize winners since the award was established early in the century.
   b. William Faulkner's Nobel Prize acceptance speech, made in 1949, contained numerous passages that one often hears quoted.
   c. The Swedish Parliament's Nobel Committee announced that the Peace Prize for 1966 would not be given for lack of a suitable candidate.

9. a. Christopher Columbus, whose real name was Cristoforo Colombo, discovered the West Indies in 1492.
   b. Columbus was not actually a Spaniard but rather an Italian who sailed for Spain.
   c. Before his departure from Spain, Christopher Columbus experienced some discouraging legal setbacks.

10. a. Christmas in Italy is a merry time of the year.
   b. On Christmas Eve, the people of the Italian town of Santa Cristina practice several famous customs.
   c. There's nothing like Christmas when it comes to Italians.

EXERCISE 5:   *Do exactly as you did in the preceding exercise.*

1. a. The Hohokam Indians lived 2,000 years ago in the southwestern United States.
   b. Arizona's ancient Hohokam Indians have strewn the desert with relics of a relatively advanced culture.
   c. The Hohokam Indians built canals to carry water for their crops.

2. a. Will success spoil Rocky Colavito?
   b. Rocky Colavito, Cleveland's great outfielder, grew up in the same New York neighborhood as Hank Greenberg.
   c. Cleveland's popular Rocky Colavito attributes his hitting success to a few simple formulas.

3. a. The Pacific islands of Micronesia constitute a United States Trust Territory.
   b. Micronesia consists of 2,100 islands, of which 96 are uninhabited.
   c. The peaceful little Micronesian islands were the setting for several of the fiercest United States-Japanese battles of World War II.

4. a. Montreal is a city with definite European characteristics.
   b. After Paris, Montreal is the second-largest French-speaking city in the world.
   c. Montreal is a huge city with a population of nearly 2,500,000.

5. a. Joseph Stalin's daughter Svetlana used her mother's maiden name, Alliluyeva, when she came to the United States for refuge.
   b. Should the United States grant refuge to Svetlana Stalin, daughter of the late Joseph Stalin?
   c. Citizens of Moscow argue that Svetlana Stalin once lived a pampered life.
6. a. On April 10, 1912, the *Titanic* left Southampton for New York.
   b. The *Titanic,* nicknamed The Millionaire's Special, was outfitted in great luxury.
   c. The disastrous trip was the *Titanic*'s maiden voyage.
7. a. OOB are the initials of a new theater movement called Off-Off-Broadway.
   b. In a typical OOB production, literally anything goes.
   c. OOB had its start around 1958.
8. a. At present, employee theft is one of U.S. industry's most expensive problems.
   b. In 1966, U.S. industry lost two billion dollars through theft by employees.
   c. Will theft become America's central moral issue of the '70's?
9. a. Irving Bedrock always has a gallon of burgundy in his car.
   b. Bedrock carries a notebook containing the name of every girl he's ever known and some he's never met.
   c. Irving Bedrock may well be the most aggressive male in New York.
10. a. Many of the prestige colleges have recently shown a preference for candidates from the public schools.
   b. Harvard accepted 1,350 out of 7,150 applicants for the 1967 fall term.
   c. Cornell had over 4,000 applications for 748 openings this year.

EXERCISE 6: *Now, we are to some extent reversing the process. This exercise provides you with a group of specific facts that have something in common. Your task is to determine the subject of that group of facts. Place it in the first blank. Then choose a descriptive word or short phrase that makes a judgment or statement about the subject. Check a dictionary to be sure that the word or phrase that you have chosen as the controlling idea is accurate. Place it in the second blank, and then give a definition of it in the following blank.*

Example: a. Two years ago, when in college, Bilkstaff earned fourteen thousand dollars per year with his research-paper service.
   b. Three months after graduation purchased the major stock in Bumble Billiard Company, a million-dollar-a-year enterprise.
   c. Soon afterward, headed the Coleman Cookie Company, a major midwestern corporation.
   d. Last year, company merged with the Remington Jelly Company, a consolidation worth several million dollars.

e. At the beginning of this fiscal year, owned four major companies, and was earning an estimated three million dollars yearly.

Subj.: *Bilkstaff's rise to fortune*   C.I.: *meteoric*
Definition of C.I.: *like a meteor; dazzling or brilliant; flashing or swift*

1. a. Lily Parsell married home-town banker at age twenty.
   b. Divorced; married Congressman at age twenty-four.
   c. At age twenty-eight, widowed; married heir to Borax fortune.
   d. Ten years later wed Panamanian playboy.
   e. Most recently, engaged to West German diplomat.

Subj.: _____ C.I.: _____
Definition of C.I.: _____

---

2. a. The Expresso, a well-known European luxury car, features sixteen selected gauges of sheet metal that form unit body.
   b. Metal is welded at ten thousand separate points along body unit.
   c. Surface is hand-sanded, filed, and inspected for several hours.
   d. Over twenty pounds of permanent undercoating are applied to protect underbody and to deaden reverberation in the metal.
   e. Thirteen coats of hand-rubbed lacquer then are applied to the finish.

Subj.: _____ C.I.: _____
Definition of C.I.: _____

---

3. a. Ernest Hemingway critically acclaimed in his early twenties for his short stories.
   b. With publication of *The Sun Also Rises,* became internationally known novelist before age thirty.
   c. Was expert amateur boxer — victorious in several bouts.
   d. Caught world-record marlin on fishing trip off South America.
   e. Military expert — consulted by famous generals.
   f. Expert biologist and botanist — had species of fish named for him.

Subj.: _____ C.I.: _____
Definition of C.I.: _____

---

4. a. Vojislav Stefanovic fought for Serbian partisans, 1943.
   b. Stefanovic imprisoned by the Tito government from 1949 to 1951 for subversive political activities.
   c. Soviet agent in Albania, 1955-57.

    d. Defected to West from Austria, 1959.

    e. Worked for British counterintelligence in the Balkans, 1961-63.

    f. Indicted by British for selling rocket specifications in Sofia, Bulgaria.

    g. Was traded to Russians for captured British agent; last seen in Budapest, 1966.

Subj.: _____ C.I.: _____

Definition of C.I.: _____

---

5. a. In the nineteenth century, whaling ship *Charles W. Morgan* operated without loss for eighty years.

    b. Earned two million dollars for her owners during active service.

    c. Caught sixty-one whales on one voyage.

    d. On a single trip in 1841, earned close to seventy thousand dollars.

Subj.: _____ C.I.: _____

Definition of C.I.: _____

---

6. a. Ellington Wrapworth was honor man at Choate, 1945.

    b. Junior class president at Harvard, 1948; age twenty.

    c. Student body president, Harvard, 1949.

    d. M.A. in law, Princeton, 1951; took position with Wall Street law firm.

    e. Special assistant to district attorney, 1955.

    f. Parks Commissioner, New York City, 1957.

Subj.: _____ C.I.: _____

Definition of C.I.: _____

---

7. a. The windows of Kensey Brundle's old place glow on summer nights with blue light.

    b. People have seen dark figures prowling about the grounds on rainy nights.

    c. Sounds of distant growling and crying come from the house during winter.

    d. Tracks of an enormous pair of hobnailed shoes found there after heavy snows.

    e. In summer, smoke sometimes rises from the chimney.

Subj.: _____ C.I.: _____

Definition of C.I.: _____

---

8. a. Milton E. Grundy, chairman of the board of Broadwhistle Industries, often shouts at subordinates, "Don't feel! Think! Thinking's what produces corporate assets."

b. Often awakens subordinates at 3:00 A.M. for facts missing from reports submitted.

c. Once screamed at junior executive, "You couldn't find your feet with both hands!"

d. Expects executives to have completely memorized all pertinent statistics when they talk to him.

e. All subordinates required to stand in his presence.

Subj.: _____ C.I.: _____

Definition of C.I.: _____

_____

9. a. Winston Kegbeer cooks excellent shish kebab for his friends.

b. Built his own home on land purchased with earnings as postman.

c. Flies a Cessna to Santa Rosa on weekends.

d. Builds furniture from walnut and maple and paints quality pictures with water colors.

e. Restores antique cars to perfect condition.

Subj.: _____ C.I.: _____

Definition of C.I.: _____

_____

10. a. After a fight with Pacific Utilities over her electric bill, Mrs. Amelia Palooka closed her account and has used kerosene lamps ever since.

b. Mrs. Palooka always tells son Fester, "If you want something done right, do it yourself."

c. Grows and cans enough fruit and vegetables to keep her larder stocked all year round.

d. When the city refused to move a huge pile of debris that had been washed by the rain off its property onto hers, Mrs. Palooka rented a bulldozer and moved it back herself.

e. Makes all her own clothing.

Subj.: _____ C.I.: _____

Definition of C.I.: _____

_____

EXERCISE 7: *Do exactly as you did in the preceding exercise.*

1. a. Al Blunt's favorite number is seven.

b. He never steps on a crack in the pavement.

c. Blunt carries a rabbit's foot.

d. He never does anything an even number of times.

Subj.: _____ C.I.: _____

Definition of C.I.: _____

_____

2. a. RAF Lieutenant Peter Wingate flew in battle of Britain, 1940.
   b. Captain Wingate was shot down in North Africa, 1942.
   c. Group Commander Wingate was shot down over Palermo, 1943.
   d. Rescued by partisans.
   e. Survivor of *Andrea-Dorea* disaster.

Subj.: _____ C.I.: _____

Definition of C.I.: _____

_____

3. a. Typical Hemingway hero is wounded man, physically and intellectually.
   b. Does not gripe or try to make excuses.
   c. A man of few words.
   d. Tries to "hold tight" and avoid crying out when in danger.
   e. When in trouble, he doesn't tell anybody.

Subj.: _____ C.I.: _____

Definition of C.I.: _____

_____

4. a. The French Minimax averages fifty miles per gallon.
   b. Goes sixty thousand miles per set of tires.
   c. Needs oil change (two quarts) once a year.
   d. Has no radiator so cannot freeze or take antifreeze.

Subj.: _____ C.I.: _____

Definition of C.I.: _____

_____

5. a. Broderick Whipple usually wears moccasins in all weather.
   b. Rides to school on Japanese motorcycle, wearing his sombrero and serape.
   c. Has black hair shoulder-length.
   d. Wears frock coat with shoulder straps.
   e. Wears paisley shirt with button reading "Nirvana Now."

Subj.: _____ C.I.: _____

Definition of C.I.: _____

_____

6. a. In a speech, college instructor Benjamin Pumpernick recently told a woman's club that it was one of the symbols of "emasculated America."

b. Always greets new classes with the statement, "Intellectually, most of you were ambushed in the nursery."

c. Told the Dean that the college dress code was "juvenile and degrading."

d. Characterized two-year college as "a high school with ash trays."

e. Wrote to the state legislature advocating that the governor be impeached.

Subj.: _____ C.I.: _____

Definition of C.I.: _____

_____

7. a. Catherine Barkeley, the heroine in Hemingway's *A Farewell to Arms,* tells her lover, "You're my religion."

b. Maria in *For Whom the Bell Tolls* says to Robert Jordan, "I am thee."

c. Renata, young countess in *Across the River and into the Trees,* wishes to sacrifice herself for Colonel Cantwell.

d. In Hemingway's *To Have and Have Not,* Harry Morgan's wife says, "God, he was a man."

Subj.: _____ C.I.: _____

Definition of C.I.: _____

_____

8. a. Ronald Rooter buys Hathaway shirts at Roos-Atkins.

b. Wears Belloni shoes from Milano.

c. His slacks are slim, tapered, from Hong Kong.

d. Has a preference for blade-thin Parisian silk ties.

e. Wears an Edinburgh vest or waistcoat during cold months.

Subj.: _____ C.I.: _____

Definition of C.I. _____

_____

9. a. In Professor Muller's class, there are usually three girls talking audibly during the lecture.

b. Half-way through the lecture, a boy enters and drags a projector across the room.

c. A man in the last row has a habit of incessantly drumming on the desk with his pencil.

d. Muller often changes the subject abruptly or else has a five-minute coughing fit.

e. Sometimes during the lecture the professor simply stares into space for three minutes at a time.

Subj.: _____ C.I.: _____

Definition of C.I.: _____

_____

10. a. Paul Pinchwick speaks admiringly of his friends.
    b. Gives credit to whoever else helped with a project.
    c. Last spring he refused to admit that he had been helping a poor family financially.
    d. Forgave two teen-agers who completely wrecked his prize greenhouse.
    e. He said, "Prosecuting them won't restore my greenhouse but could hurt them in the future."

Subj.: _____ C.I.: _____

Definition of C.I.: _____

EXERCISE 8: *Devise a topic sentence to accommodate each set of facts listed below. Take time to ensure that the controlling idea points toward the facts and that it accounts for all the facts.*

1. a. Andrew Soupwell has at least three hundred thousand dollars invested in San Francisco theatrical ventures.
   b. He owns a view apartment building in the Golden Gateway.
   c. He is a member of the New York Stock Exchange.
   d. Soupwell, a 40-year-old bachelor, also owns the controlling interest in a professional football team in the NFL.

   _____

   _____

   _____

2. a. Patagonia, occupying the southern part of Argentina in South America, has a long winter and a cold and arid climate.
   b. Trees and shrubs on the bleak plains are stunted and bent over by wind and drought.
   c. Scrub grass and thistle bushes are the predominant ground covering.
   d. Although Patagonia makes up one-fifth of the total land area of Argentina, it contains less than 3 percent of the population.
   e. In this land near the tip of the Western Hemisphere, stockades twenty feet high surround the developments to protect the inhabitants and the sheep from wind and wild pumas.

   _____

   _____

   _____

20

3. a. Eleven months ago in Chicago, Gregorio Panatela began a long winning streak by knocking out fourth-ranked welterweight Del Brooks with a left hook in the last minute of the fifth round.
   b. Three weeks later Panatela won a decision over Artie Ponchatrain, the leading welterweight contender, in a ten-round bout held in New Orleans.
   c. Panatela waited four months to score his next victory, a seventh-round knockout of Peruvian welterweight champion Bartolo Ledesma in Lima.
   d. Last month he won a decision over world champion Harvey Bromo in a nontitle ten-rounder in Madison Square Garden.

_____

_____

_____

4. a. The Bay Area's largest horse-racing track, Golden Gate Fields, has four cocktail lounges, four restaurants, nine refreshment stands, and five stand-up bars.
   b. As a convenience, escalators have been installed to carry people from the clubhouse and the grandstand to the paddock.
   c. The entrances to the cocktail lounges are draped in green and white satin, and the club is carpeted throughout in matching green.
   d. There are two private entrances where valets are stationed to park the patrons' cars.

_____

_____

_____

5. a. In 1948, Freemuth Frisbull became the second high-school student in history to run one hundred yards in 9.4 seconds.
   b. Frisbull also was All-State in football, scoring twenty-one touchdowns in his senior year.
   c. Frisbull lettered in football, baseball, track, and boxing his sophomore year in college, at which time he was chosen to the NCAA All-American baseball team as center fielder.
   d. Frisbull was Olympic decathlon champion two years after graduating from college.
   e. Last year, at the age of thirty-seven, Frisbull won the Amateur Outdoor Tennis Championship of the Pacific Northwest.

_____

_____

_____

6. a. Angel Island, in San Francisco Bay, has miles of hiking trails winding through semi-wilderness.
   b. Eventually, when it is made a state park, it will have thousands of picnic tables for family use.
   c. It has two swimming beaches.
   d. It has docking space for 471 boats and camping sites for 1,900 families at one time.
   e. A small mountain in the center of the island provides a striking view of the surrounding area.

_____

_____

_____

7. a. Guide-dog puppies are farmed out to selected 4-H Club youngsters in whose homes the pups learn basic obedience, become accustomed to children, and are housebroken.
   b. Potential guide dogs for the blind must learn early to ride in cars and to accept affection from other people.
   c. For three to five months they must be trained rigorously in avoiding obstacles.
   d. Before they are entrusted to guiding the blind, the dogs must learn to contend with ditches, dropped objects, revolving doors, flights of stairs, and traffic.

_____

_____

_____

8. a. A visitor in Lisbon can rent a room in one of Europe's finest hotels for as little as $12.00 per day.
   b. There are many boarding houses throughout Portugal where one can get clean lodgings and tasty meals for $3.50 daily.
   c. A Portuguese meal of bread, cheese, olives, and a bottle of good red wine costs as little as $1.00 in American money.
   d. A tasty domestic beer can be purchased for 15 cents per bottle in most Portuguese cantinas.

_____

_____

_____

9. a. Detroit's automobiles in the near future will be equipped with more interior padding than ever before.
   b. General Motors and American Motors both have plans for a collapsible steering column that folds up in a collision.
   c. Detroit planners are already designing models with front-seat room large enough to permit a person's head to jerk forward without striking the dashboard during a collision.
   d. General Motors and American Motors have three-way taillights on the designing boards: these lights are green when the driver's foot is on the accelerator, amber when the accelerator pedal is released, and the usual red when the driver brakes.

_____

_____

_____

10. a. The U.S. Office of Education estimates that by 1975 nine million students will be enrolled in U.S. colleges, three million more than there are today.
    b. Within twenty years, one expert estimates, every existing school will be at least double in size.
    c. By 1985, 1,000 new colleges will be created to accommodate people desiring a higher education.
    d. One school estimates that in eight years enrollment alone will increase from 6,600 to 10,000.

_____

_____

_____

EXERCISE 9:   *Do exactly as you did in the preceding exercise.*

1. a. Last year in Alabama, a Negro named Lucius Amerson defeated a white opponent in an election for sheriff of a county.
   b. In San Francisco in 1966, Willie Brown, who is a Negro, won a seat in the Eighteenth Congressional District to set a local political precedent.
   c. Edward Brooke, Republican Attorney General of Massachusetts, became a Senator in 1966.
   d. Brooke, the first Negro Senator since Reconstruction, is considered by his party to possess excellent vice-presidential potential.

2. a. Political columnist Walter Winchell characterized William Manchester's long-awaited book *The Death of a President* as having "neither elegance nor grandeur."
   b. Allistair Cook suggested that Manchester himself lacks "almost everything hitherto prescribed for contemporary historians."
   c. One reviewer felt that the book was too detailed.
   d. Gore Vidal called Manchester "starry-eyed" for ever agreeing in the first place to write an "official version" of the assassination.
   e. Tom Wicker said that as the book went along, it "grew aimlessly fatter and fatter."

3. a. Svetlana Stalin's brother Jacob died as a captive of the Nazis in World War II.
   b. Her other brother, Vasily, died in 1962 under mysterious circumstances.
   c. When Svetlana Stalin was sixteen, she discovered that her mother's death had been a suicide rather than one by natural causes.
   d. Her husband, an Indian named Brajish Singh, was discriminated against in the Soviet Union and died there.
   e. Svetlana's father Joseph Stalin was, after his death, discredited and reviled in the Soviet Union.

4. a. Women shoplifters sometimes wear a device called booster bloomers, oversized bloomers into which stolen articles can be dropped.
   b. A false-bottom purse will hold jewelry and other small items.
   c. An umbrella is also fine for storing small pilfered items.
   d. Some women shoplifters spirit out small pieces of jewelry in their shoes, gloves, and even under their hats.

5. a. Most "singles-only" apartments feature swimming pools, tennis courts, and basement gymnasiums and provide free instruction in coed golf, tennis, and ballroom dancing.
   b. One singles-only apartment complex features joint discussion groups for intellectual young men and women who wouldn't be likely to meet one another at dances.
   c. The entrance requirements for a young woman are that she be single and reasonably pretty.
   d. Most of the young bachelors who live there are college educated and work in a professional capacity.
   e. In one singles-only apartment complex, a few years ago, four bachelor roommates married four young women who were also roommates.

6. a. In his efforts to revise the California abortion law of 1861, Senator Anthony Beilenson recently argued that his pending therapeutic abortion bill would replace a nineteenth-century act that drove "thousands of women to their deaths every year."
   b. According to the *San Francisco Chronicle,* he called the old law "archaic," since it was passed before women could vote in California.
   c. Senator Beilenson labeled the old bill "hypocritical," because violators— physicians and the women involved—were seldom prosecuted.
   d. The Senator also said the old bill was barbaric, for it forced women to seek out quacks instead of allowing them to receive the professional care they needed.

7. a. Around Lake Tahoe, large areas that have been paved into streets and parking lots prevent melting snow from being absorbed by the earth and cause it to flow off into the lake, raising its normal level.
   b. Street sweepings and salt used for melting road ice flow into the lake, killing some kinds of marine life.

c. Fertilizers from golf courses and the issue from countless septic tanks also end up in Lake Tahoe.

d. Denuded hillsides, cut up by construction bulldozers, drain their mud into the lake water.

_____

_____

_____

8. a. In 1810 George Gordon, Lord Byron, swam the Hellespont, a treacherous strait that separates Europe from Asia.

b. At twenty-three years of age, upon earning world literary fame for his first two published works, Lord Byron gave away all his royalties in order to maintain his image as "an aristocratic amateur."

c. In the next few years, Byron was active—in the House of Lords as an extreme political liberal and friend of the dispossessed, in the town as a man whom women could not leave alone.

d. A scandal involving Byron and his half-sister Augusta Leigh forced him to leave England for good in 1816.

e. In 1824 Byron organized and led a group of fighting men to assist the Greeks in their war against the Turks.

f. Byron died of fever in Missolonghi, Greece, just after his thirty-sixth birthday.

_____

_____

_____

9. a. Stored blood, so crucial to life-preserving transfusions, can be kept only about three weeks before the red cells disintegrate.

b. The white cells in stored blood can often cause a sensitization reaction in a patient, which results in chills, fever, and even death in rare cases.

c. Hepatitis virus hiding in stored blood can transmit the dangerous serum hepatitis to transfusion patients.

d. Donors of rare blood types sometimes cannot be found in time to help patients who have lost excessive blood in accidents.

e. Person-to-person transfusions are not often practicable.

_____

_____

_____

10. a. In a typical supper-club performance, comedian Marty Melon is likely to yell, "Dig the nose on the guy coming in. He could hire out as a bloodhound."
    b. When a lady accidentally spilled some of her cocktail during one of his performances, Melon asked, "Been drinking long, honey?"
    c. Melon always tells his audiences, "You think you're rating *me*. But I've been rating you, and I just laid the lowest score this month on you."
    d. He once quipped to an entering celebrity with a wide reputation for wife-stealing, "Hey, Bennie, go home. All the girls here are single."

_____

_____

_____

EXERCISE 10: *Choose one of the following topic sentences and then write a 100-200 word paragraph supporting it as factually as you can. Try not to rely solely on memory for the facts. Consult outside sources such as books, magazines, and newspapers for information, or else use actual observation.*

1. Even outside the ring, ex-heavyweight boxing champion Cassius Clay made headlines with his actions.
2. The late President John F. Kennedy is especially remembered for his humor and his warmth.
3. During the course of his Hollywood screen career, Marlon Brando has portrayed a series of rough, individualistic characters.
4. The Volkswagen is in many respects an economical car to operate.
5. Enrolling for a semester in college can be an expensive undertaking.
6. At the beginning of the semester, Mr. _____ , my _____ _____ instructor, discussed in detail the aims and requirements of the course.
7. The library of this college has an extensive selection of material for the study of_____ .
8. It is fascinating to note the distinctive features of this season's coed fashions.
9. The names of many of today's popular entertainment groups show originality and imagination.
10. Despite their protests to the contrary, the mode of dress of most hippies on this campus tends to be pretty uniform.

2 Unity

Unity is a word you are certain to encounter in most books on writing. Defined most simply, unity might be called "the quality of oneness," a union of related parts that form a harmonious whole. As such, unity is found in many different aspects of the civilized world, in such unrelated forms as philosophies, symphonies, office buildings, patterns of offense on the football field, suspension bridges, political party policies, and even well-planned dinners. Good writing, too, requires unity of structure, whether that writing takes the form of a novel, a complex essay, or even a single paragraph.

What is unity in writing and how does it work in a paragraph? Often, an effective way to define an object or quality is to begin by showing what it is *not.* The following student paragraph could serve as a case in point:

(1) To me the most outstanding feature of Cerebros College is the athletic department. (2) This feature makes Cerebros different from the college that I attended in the past. (3) The athletics there were in sorry shape. (4) But here at Cerebros the athletic performances are real exciting. (5) I don't think a college would amount to much if it didn't have an intramural athletic program. (6) These after-school activities help in many ways. (7) They help raise funds for other school activities and give the

student something to do besides just studying. (8) I definitely think that the student should study, granted, but he must also have fun at social events and dances. (9) The girl I go with I met at a co-rec dance. (10) In conclusion, the student shouldn't just come to school to be there, but so that he or she can participate in its functions.

Now whatever we might say about the paragraph above, we could never stretch our imaginations enough to call it organized or unified. Let's examine it in brief detail.

In his topic sentence, the writer promises us that he will discuss the outstanding qualities of the physical education department of the college. But it isn't long before he is wandering from his prescribed subject. In sentence 2, he informs us that he's had experience at a different college, but that bit of information hardly proves that Cerebros has a good athletic department. Sentences 4 and 5 deal with the writer's opinion, but not with any factual evidence in support of his "promise." By sentence 6, the writer has forgotten that he's "plugging" the physical education department, and he begins to lecture on the benefits of extra-curricular activities for the student: they raise funds for *more* extra-curricular activities, and they insure against the student's becoming stale through over-studying. Sentence 9 discusses the writer's romantic life and has little, apparently, to do with the P.E. department at Cerebros. Since the writer fails to include one convincing *fact* in support of the topic sentence, it soon becomes obvious to the impatient reader that he has been taken on a tour by a rambling mind. Let's review at a glance the unrelated areas covered in this student's paragraph:

1. The writer's educational experience at an out-of-state college.
2. The poorness of the athletic program at his former school.
3. The benefits to be derived from after-school activities (personal for the student—financial for the school).
4. Recommendations on how the student can avoid excessive study.
5. How the writer found romance at Cerebros.

Obviously, if the ideal paragraph should develop in detail only one of the areas mentioned above, this paragraph falls short of that ideal. Like many beginning students, the writer has thrown his mind into neutral and let his pen idle on. His tour has resulted in something resembling an accident; that's the kindest thing one can say about the paragraph.

But fortunately the above student revised his opening paragraph. Later in the semester he was able to produce the following example:

(1) Each week of the semester, the P.E. department at Cerebros provides the student with many chances to enjoy healthful recreation. (2) On Monday and Wednesday evenings there is co-rec dancing from seven until ten under the direction of Mrs. Bell, who sometimes teaches the students some Balkan dances. (3) Tuesdays at eight, Mr. Gardner conducts physical

exercise classes for the men, while Miss Tillotson teaches the coeds how to remain fit. (4) Tuesdays also feature intramural basketball in the main gym during the winter months and badminton or tennis on the outdoor courts in the spring when the evenings are longer. (5) The P.E. department also welcomes students to the "Friday Flicks," shown free of admission in the main gym all during the school year. (6) As can be seen, there is a weekly recreational event offered to suit nearly every preference.

Several characteristics of this revision make it more effective than the original paragraph. For one thing, the writer has made the main part of each sentence (see underlining) relate to the controlling idea of the paragraph, "healthful recreation." By so doing, he has avoided skipping around to interesting but unrelated subjects that distract the reader's attention from the major issue of the paragraph.

As a rule of thumb, unity is achieved by relating the *main clause* of each supporting sentence directly to the controlling idea of the topic sentence. Allow no sentence in the paragraph to deviate from that pattern. If you have an intriguing sentence or an idea that does not relate directly to the controlling idea, suppress your passion by setting aside the sentence, at least temporarily. Perhaps it may still be used. Later in this chapter, you will find out how to use material that is somewhat related to the subject but not strictly unified with the controlling idea of the paragraph.

Main Clause Unity

At this point, we will quickly review the difference between a main (independent) clause and a dependent one, since good unity depends, for the most part, upon main clauses being related to the topic sentence. You'll probably remember from past experience that a *clause* is a group of words that contains a subject and a verb (underlined in the following examples, with one line beneath the subject and two beneath the verb):

1. After Grabowski played lacrosse at Wisconsin in the thirties
2. Tarzan could spare some time from fighting evil.
3. Whenever Sam Suggins got liquored up
4. He ought to take a course in public speaking.
5. Since in the sorority it isn't considered polite to swear

The above constructions are clauses, all right. But they are not all main (independent) clauses. Examples 2 and 4 are independent, for they can stand by themselves with no help needed. But examples 1, 3, and 5 are dependent (subordinate) clauses; the beginning word in each—a subordinator—warns the reader that he is dealing with a construction that cannot stand by itself. Take a perfectly healthy sentence:

Tarzan could spare some time from fighting evil.

Obviously, such a group of words is perfectly capable of standing alone. But just place a subordinator in front of it, and look what happens:

If Tarzan could spare some time from fighting evil

Now, of course, you have caused what was once an independent construction to need help from something else. If you don't find help for the clause, it becomes a fragment, a construction you've probably heard discussed in the course already.

To return for a moment to the Ape Man, let's suppose the topic of the paragraph you were writing dealt with Tarzan's social shortcomings and how they could be overcome. You might aid the original clause in the following manner:

If Tarzan could spare some time from fighting evil, he'd do well to take a course in public speaking.

or, to reverse the order,

Tarzan ought to take a course in public speaking *whenever* he can spare some time from fighting evil.

Notice that it makes no difference where the subordinate clause is placed. It can begin or end the sentence. It can even come in the middle. The important point is that the *main* (independent) part of the sentence is the part that proves or supports the controlling idea, and in the above example the controlling idea expresses Tarzan's need for social sophistication. We are not directly concerned, therefore, with his fight against evil, although it makes an interesting *lesser* detail. You needn't throw it away in disgust. But you must place it out of the way of the real business of the paragraph as promised in the controlling idea. In short, subordinate Tarzan's fight against evil to his need for social improvement and you'll keep your paragraph unified, with all the main ideas supporting the controlling idea.

For a better idea of what can happen when a writer gets careless with clauses, let's look at a paragraph that was criticized by an instructor for lacking unity:

(1) Although it has yet to top Chevrolet sales, the Mustang has [greatly increased Ford's business] in the last year. (2) Accounting for 6 percent of all 1965 U.S. auto sales, the Mustang owed its success to sleek lines and "personal" tailoring. (3) Since it provided the Ford Company with 29 percent of its yearly sales, Mustang is back on the drawing boards for slight modifications which could improve it. (4) The new Mustang, which experts predict will account for at least 10 percent of the nation's sales, will feature a slightly longer hood and a shorter rear deck. (5) Engine power will also increase in keeping with the trend toward more get-away. (6) All in all, the Mustang has remade Ford Motor Company.

Not bad for a student paragraph, you are probably thinking. And you have a point. The paragraph is a bit underdeveloped, but it's literate and clearly phrased. Yet, if we all agree that the controlling idea is the promise the writer makes the reader, we'll have to admit that in this paragraph a contract has been broken. For the controlling idea—*greatly increased Ford's business*—is not directly supported in the paragraph. True, there are certain statistics provided that relate to the topic sentence, but instead of boldly appearing in main clauses of each sentence, these pertinent facts turn up, like poor cousins, in dependent constructions. The main clauses (underlined in the paragraph) seem to support some other idea. You might, for instance, try checking each clause underlined in the above paragraph against either of the following topic sentences:

> This year's Mustang will closely duplicate the styling that made it famous in 1965.
> Few changes will be made next year in Mustang's famous look.

But, alas, these ideas are not what the writer promised he was going to develop.

Again, let us remember that support for the topic sentence should be provided in main (independent) clauses in the paragraph. So if the writer decides that a new set of facts is more exciting than his original set, then he must change his topic sentence to control the new facts. Had the above student, for instance, really wished to write about the style of the Mustang, he should have constructed his topic sentence to that purpose and then used facts that would have illustrated the idea of style. Then, he should have placed those supporting facts in main clauses, not in the dependent clauses. Now compare the student's original paragraph with a revised version in which subjects and predicates have been underlined, that the instructor became so excited over that he mounted it on the wall of his office:

> (1) Although it has yet to top Chevrolet, the Mustang has provided Ford Motor Company with [some impressive sales] over the past year. (2) Owing much of its appeal to sleek lines and "personal" tailoring, the Mustang accounted for 6 percent of all U.S. auto sales in 1965. (3) Twenty-nine percent of Ford's own total sales were Mustangs, a fact that has prompted the company to make few modifications in a style that the public approved of. (4) Since reaction to this car has been so great, the Mustang alone could gain 10 percent of all American sales next year, according to financial experts. (5) A slightly longer and more powerful Mustang could earn Ford millions of dollars more in 1967. (6) Mustang popularity, then, has helped Ford Motor Company close the sales gap on Chevrolet.

You might argue that the revised version is not drastically different from its original. And again you'd have a point. Actually, many of the same facts and statistics have been used to "prove" the topic sentence in the rewrite. The difference is that in the revision, the important facts and statistics have been repositioned in the main clauses, instead of being placed in the dependent parts of sentences.

To test main clause unity, the student might try underlining the subject and verb in the main clause of each of his own sentences as we have above, using one line under the subject and two under the verb or predicate. If the independent clauses of each sentence relate directly to the controlling idea, the writer has probably achieved a reasonable degree of unity. Do you remember that "quality of oneness," that "harmonious whole" we made such an issue over at the beginning of this chapter? Well, the above paragraph begins to move toward that ideal.

Gaining Unity Through Subordination

To a certain extent, we have been discussing the concept of *subordination* in the above examples. Subordination might be defined most simply as the placing of certain ideas in less important positions than other ideas in the sentence. A subordinate clause or phrase, like a subordinate rank in military service, is a part that depends upon another more responsible part for support or direction. A subordinate construction is usually of less weight or significance than the part that it helps qualify or modify. Consider the following three short sentences:

1. Sergeant Hawkins crossed the bamboo thicket.
2. He darted to the top of a small incline.
3. At the top he was struck in the foot by a sniper's bullet.

If one were writing about the above experience, which sentence would he want to emphasize as the most significant or important? Most people, of course, would choose sentence 3; it's the climax of this set of events, and it describes the injury—perhaps serious—of a soldier. Therefore, sentences 1 and 2 are of less weight and import here. If the writer were faced with the task of fitting all three of those short sentences into a single more sophisticated sentence, then, how might he arrange them? One possibility might be the following:

> After Sergeant Hawkins crossed a bamboo thicket and started to the top of a small incline, he was struck in the foot by a sniper's bullet.

What has the writer done in this instance with sentences 1 and 2? How have they been positioned in relation to sentence 3? They may be said to have been *subordinated* (placed in a position of less importance) to sentence 3. Sentences 1 and 2 have been blended into a single clause that the writer has then made a

34

dependent by placing it after a subordinator (*After*). By subordinating these two short clauses to the more important one, the writer has positioned all these individual ideas in proper relation to one another—"first things first," "proper thoughts in proper places," and such wisdom as that.

Now to the student, subordination may not seem, at first glance, to have much to do with unity. Yet, if the writer of the following paragraph had known as much as you now know about subordination, he probably wouldn't have been penalized for lack of unity:

> (1) The nation's gullibility for unidentified flying object stories is a lucrative source of income for their authors. (2) The book *Flying Saucers— Serious Business* achieved success as a best seller. (3) Three months later John Fuller wrote a book called *Incident at Exeter.* (4) It was just as profitable as *Flying Saucers—Serious Business.* (5) So Fuller wrote an article entitled "Aboard a Flying Saucer." (6) This was an account of a couple who claimed they had been taken aboard a saucer and questioned. (7) Fuller sold the article to *Look* magazine. (8) Barney and Betty Hill were the couple in Fuller's article. (9) They received $24,000 for their story. (10) Mr. Fuller and Dr. Benjamin Simon plan to split the profits from a future book or movie based on the experiences of the Hills. (11) Dr. Simon is a noted psychiatrist from Boston, and he analyzed the Hills. (12) Flying saucers make good business these days.

Not much analysis is needed to see rather quickly that the controlling idea (*lucrative source of income*) is not supported in every sentence that follows it. Sentences 2, 4, 7, 9, and 10 all seem to support the promise, since each of these sentences reports a profit made by one person or another from writings about flying saucers. But what about sentences 3, 5, 6, 8, and 11? Should the writer take the easy way out and get rid of these unrelated sentences? In this instance, the writer refused to be defeated. He remembered that it was permissible to incorporate into a paragraph material that was not directly related to the topic sentence. He simply subordinated the sentences that didn't report a profit to those that did. The result is the following student revision:

> (1) The nation's gullibility for unidentified flying object stories and sightings is a lucrative source of income for their authors. (2) For example, the book *Flying Saucers—Serious Business,* written early this year by former radio-businessman Frank Edwards, achieved remarkable success as a big seller. (3) Three months later, *Saturday Review* writer John Fuller's *Incident at Exeter* was as popular as Mr. Edwards' book. (4) As a result of this success, Mr. Fuller sold *Look* magazine a follow-up article entitled, "Aboard a Flying Saucer," an account of a couple questioned in a flying saucer. (5) Betty and Barney Hill, the couple in Fuller's article, also profited from the publication, having thus far received $24,000 for their story. (6) Finally, Mr. Fuller and Dr. Benjamin Simon, the noted Boston psychiatrist who analyzed the Hills, plan to share the

profits from a book or movie proposed for 1967 and based on the Hills' experience. (7) Judging from these examples, it wouldn't seem like a bad bet to try a UFO story of one's own.

Notice the ways in which the revision improves upon the original:

1. Most importantly, it focuses all the independent clauses upon the controlling idea, making the paragraph unified. (You might try underlining the subject and verbs in the main clauses and running a check of your own).
2. It cuts down the number of sentences from twelve to seven.
3. It avoids all the repetition we find in the original paragraph.
4. It smooths the flow of the prose, making the writing less choppy by using certain transitional phrases that we will discuss further on.

You'll probably admit that subordination was worth trying in the above writer's case. The returns in better prose were worth his investment of time. What resulted was writing that was more "muscular," since the writer compressed his paragraph through subordination. Subordination, then, helps achieve unity, to be sure. But in addition it can also help the student to cut the fat out of his writing, to work his prose into solid bone and muscle. And who wouldn't enjoy being stronger in one way or another?

Summary: Unity

1. Unity occurs in a paragraph in which all the sentences of the paragraph relate to the controlling idea and fulfill its "promise."
2. Strict unity is best achieved by relating the main clause of each supporting sentence to the controlling idea of the topic sentence.
3. If the writer wishes to use in his paragraph ideas that are not directly related to the main idea, he should position these ideas in subordinate clauses or phrases. Then they may be included in the paragraph.
4. To test main clause unity, the student should underline the subject and verb of each main clause and check these against the controlling idea of the paragraph.

EXERCISE 11:   *All but one of the sentences in each of the following groups have a common subject and would constitute a unified paragraph. Pick the sentence that does not belong in this paragraph and place the letter of that sentence in the first blank. In the second blank, summarize the topic that unifies the remaining sentences.*

1. a. In several eastern European countries last year, cold early rains drowned much of the seed in farmers' fields.
   b. Hail storms along the Danube Valley flattened young plants.
   c. Floods in Poland took their toll of new crops, which washed away in the waters.
   d. A lack of modern machinery compounded last year's difficulties in many eastern European countries.
   e. Locusts ate vast portions of the wheat crop in the Ukraine.

_____

2. a. Sugar Ray Robinson missed repeatedly with his jab in early rounds against Joey Archer in Madison Square Garden last week.
   b. By the third round, Archer was hitting Robinson almost at will with jabs and crosses.
   c. Archer used a combination jab and cross in the middle rounds to harass the veteran fighter.
   d. The 45-year-old Sugar Ray began his ring career when Archer was two years old.
   e. Archer found the range with a hook once or twice in the late rounds, but failed to down Robinson.

_____

3. a. One of last season's soap commercials depicted a washing machine growing ten feet tall when the sponsor's product was used.
   b. In another ad, a knight on a white stallion cleans dirty clothes simply by galloping by and pointing his lance at terrified people.
   c. In a cleanser ad, a woman floats out through the window bearing the product in her hand.
   d. Another ad depicts a giant made of soapsuds who crushes and destroys a villainous-looking character called "Mr. Greene."
   e. Most of these ads feature music as well as a slight drama.

_____

4. a. Today in eastern Europe, only one out of four 1957 Polish-built Syrena automobiles is still in running condition.
   b. There is a great shortage of spare parts for any make of car in Russia and the satellite countries.
   c. American cars are not sold in Yugoslavia, Poland, Russia, Hungary, or Czechoslovakia.
   d. Out of 1,500 gas stations in Russia only 63 stay open twenty-four hours a day.
   e. In Moscow, there are only eight garages available to service over seventy thousand automobiles.

_____

5. a. The late President Woodrow Wilson's Ph.D. thesis "Congressional Government" was an original study of comparative political institutions.
   b. In 1887 Wilson's article "The Study of Administration" interested students in a growing government.
   c. "Constitutional Government in the United States," a treatise composed from Wilson's lectures at Columbia, is still studied with interest in the United States.
   d. Sigmund Freud and William C. Bullitt, however, dismiss much of Wilson's writing as "beautiful but empty rhetoric."
   e. Wilson's book *The State* is still used in the classroom.

---

6. a. All across Mexico—from Sinaloa to Oaxaca—iguana lizards provide game for the sportsman carrying small-arms weapons.
   b. Hunters who wish to bring their own guns into Mexico are required to procure from the Mexican consulate a certificate of good conduct, which costs sixteen dollars.
   c. In Baja, around Mulege and Loreto, duck and quail hunting with shotgun is excellent during the spring months.
   d. The prehistoric-looking tapir can be hunted in the marshy jungles of the south.
   e. For the hunter carrying large-bore firearms, the grizzly of the forests above Hermosillo is the big challenge.

---

7. a. Last season, in his first year as a pro, Los Angeles' Bruno Prewicz gained 237 yards from scrimmage in a game against the Bears.
   b. He scored twenty-one touchdowns to establish a new NFL record.
   c. Prewicz was a three-time All-American from Penn State.
   d. In a game with the Steelers in the Los Angeles Coliseum, Prewicz scored on sprints of 67, 82, 83, and 91 yards respectively.
   e. In a game with the Cardinals, Prewicz caught a 20-yard flat pass and outran the whole defense to score the winning touchdown.

---

8. a. Some men seek adventure like big-game hunting out of a competitive instinct, a need to assert themselves.
   b. Some are loners who prefer the autonomy of lion-taming.
   c. Others challenge "killer" mountains out of egocentricity.
   d. Still others admit that cave-exploring or scuba-diving adds point and meaning and even a touch of zest to living.
   e. Most adventurers will readily agree, however, that no undertaking is quite so hazardous as marriage.

---

9. a. Sir Francis Chichester, the famed British yacht skipper, had his automatic steering device smashed by giant seas about seventy-five days out of England.
   b. A day out of Sydney, Australia, Chichester's craft was almost flipped over on its side by 75-knot winds.
   c. By this time, Chichester had set a record by sailing farther than any lone mariner ever had without a sight of land.
   d. After he rounded Cape Horn and headed home to England, Chichester found he was running low on supplies, and he also developed an abscess in his elbow and had to take a pain-killer.

_____ _____

10. a. In one of the most successful TV series of recent years, the main character is a young man who is dying slowly of an incurable disease.
    b. The young man, who remains vigorous despite the illness, is a former lawyer and assistant district attorney from San Francisco.
    c. He is also a former Air Force pilot who flew in combat in Korea.
    d. The young man is handsome and appealing to pretty girls, who turn up regularly on the show.
    e. Something new will have to be added to the young man's attributes, if the show is expected to survive another year.

_____ _____

EXERCISE 12:   *Do exactly as you did in the preceding exercise.*

1. a. E. Harvey Pummel's commitments to charity amount to about twenty thousand dollars annually.
   b. Pummel is the secretary of Friends of the Opera in his city, and through his time and monetary contributions he has helped make the symphony orchestra a successful venture.
   c. He is a generous friend to his church and has even preached occasionally as a lay minister.
   d. Pummel, who is president of a large manufacturing company, neither smokes nor drinks, and he disapproves strongly of gambling.
   e. He personally lent his name and office to a campaign last year to collect money for benefits for disabled children.

_____ _____

2. a. Statistics reveal that annual worldwide food production increased by 1 to 1½ percent while population explodes upwards to 2 percent.
   b. In California, prime agricultural land is being paved over at the rate of 375 acres per day.

c. "Already, automobiles occupy more space in America than people do," reports Edward Crafts of the U.S. Bureau of Outdoor Recreation.

d. In order to stay above the starvation level, we will have to double the world's food production in the next three decades, it has been estimated.

e. We will need to quadruple it within the next half century.

---

3. a. At Georgetown University, students voted five to one to increase the length of their vacations as a safety valve to release pressure built up by the academic grind.

b. At the University of Colorado, four thousand out of nearly sixteen thousand registered students seek help each year from the psychologists at the university's counseling service.

c. A Harvard psychologist estimates that each year 10 percent of the student body requires his help.

d. Eight to ten percent of Northwestern's total student enrollment has gone to the university's psychiatric counseling office annually for the last few years.

e. At Wisconsin, an estimated fifteen thousand hours of psychotherapy each year helps keep the suicide rate relatively low for a large university.

---

4. a. "The human knee was never meant for a game like football," said an NFL quarterback after tearing out knee ligaments in a Sunday game.

b. A linebacker in the AFL has had seven operations on both knees over the past six years—and continues to play.

c. The knee is held together mainly by ligaments and cartilage and is not well adapted to the sorts of sidewise contact it frequently receives on the pro gridiron.

d. Joe Namath, the bonus rookie of the New York Jets, needed major knee surgery before he ever played a full season in the pros.

e. Unlike the knee, the shoulder and the hip are fastened by powerful ball-and-socket joints that can be twisted or flexed in several directions without undue strain.

---

5. a. Some critics believe that a 30-day "cooling-off" period before the issuance of a license would make marriage more difficult to enter into and thus more precious.

b. San Jose State sociologist Mervyn Cadwallader believes in establishing marriage on a flexible contract basis—one or two years with occasional options to renew if both parties are satisfied.

c. Last year alone, three hundred forty thousand divorce actions were begun by U.S. wives.

d. A famous sociologist believes in a marital contract that would allow partners to decide at the outset not to have children.

e. Several well-known sociologists believe that a marriage based upon the intentions of founding a family should require both partners to agree to this in writing beforehand.

_____

6. a. Among some under-sea treasures recently recovered in one hundred feet of water in the Bahamas is a silver crucifix two inches long.

b. Recovering treasure at such depths involves great risks to divers using scuba equipment.

c. Porcelain cups in perfect condition were found on a wreck in Puerto Rico.

d. A long chain of polished gold links was found in the Philippines.

e. Several thousand dollars worth of Spanish coins were taken from a wreck in thirty feet of water off the California coast near Moss Landing.

_____

7. a. In parts of California, many stands of scenic, thousand-year-old red-woods are in danger of being harvested by lumber interests.

b. These trees have relatively shallow roots that like the slopes of deep canyons, where the trees find shelter from the winds.

c. Redwoods require heavy irrigation by rains from November through April.

d. To achieve maturity, the giant sequoias need fog, which the trees absorb as moisture.

e. The sequoia redwoods prefer the black alluvial soil found in parts of northern California and southern Oregon.

_____

8. a. The late West German Chancellor Konrad Adenauer was the man responsible for bringing Germany into the Atlantic Alliance.

b. Adenauer, who fully acknowledged Germany's guilt in the genocide of six million European Jews, arranged seven billion dollars' worth of reparations for survivors and their families.

c. Adenauer accomplished a treaty of friendship between old enemies, France and Germany.

d. In ten years of shrewd political leadership, he turned his nation into the third largest industrial state in the world.

e. Even as mayor of Cologne in the early thirties, Adenauer was openly and publically against the rise of Nazism.

_____

9. a. It is estimated that by 1975 the U.S. government will serve people of all ages with a complete medical coverage resembling Medicare, with clinics in every town in the nation and massive hospitals in major cities.
   b. At present, in many of the major hospitals, mechanized artificial limbs of great versatility are being developed.
   c. Doctors in major hospitals are working on an exam that reveals ahead of time potentially cancerous cells.
   d. Artificial kidneys are presently being tested to determine if they can be transplanted in human beings.
   e. Instruments that can see inside the organs will soon replace exploratory surgery in up-to-date hospitals.

10. a. Republican mayor George Potluck of Quaker Heights believes strongly in catering to the business community and favors the interests of capital above those of labor.
    b. Mayor Potluck approves heartily of U.S. participation in the war in Vietnam.
    c. Potluck, a member of the board of trustees at the local college, is opposed to much emphasis on the liberal arts such as literature, philosophy, and history. "Give them meat and potato courses," he says.
    d. The mayor is a lover of symphonic music and is so knowledgeable about it that he lectures on Beethoven and Mozart.
    e. He backed Arizona Senator Barry Goldwater in the 1964 elections and vigorously campaigned for California Governor Ronald Reagan in 1966.
    f. The mayor personally led a movement to drive all "bohemian elements" out of Quaker Heights.

EXERCISE 13:   *Do exactly as you did in the preceding exercise.*

1. a. Ace automobile racer Archie Magwirth finished a race at Detroit last year with huge blisters on his hands from gripping the wheel so savagely.
   b. Magwirth, who is from Leeds, England, broke his left leg in a pile-up at the fairgrounds in Reading, Pennsylvania.
   c. Three months later he was badly burned at Dayton when the cockpit wiring of his midget auto caught fire.
   d. In April of last year, Magwirth was the leading money winner when he flipped his car at Fort Worth and suffered a broken right arm.
   e. He still would have finished the season driving one-handed if he hadn't needed sudden surgery for appendicitis in Waukegan.

2. a. Major Marcus A. Reno, the scapegoat for the disastrous defeat at the Little Big Horn, once broke a cue stick over the head of another officer during a hard-drinking evening.
   b. Reno was court-martialed for looking through a parlor window one night at his commanding officer's daughter, whom he admired very much.
   c. On the day of George Custer's defeat and death at the Little Big Horn in 1876, Major Reno led his forces successfully against a Sioux party about four miles away and did not come to Custer's aid.
   d. In 1879, Reno was accused of paying court to the wife of another officer.
   e. On another occasion, an enraged Reno broke a chair against the window of a billiard room.

---

3. a. After taking a Vietnamese village, the first task Colonel William James and his men had was to rebuild a ruined bridge.
   b. They reopened a store that had been closed for a year.
   c. The store had closed when the owner was intimidated by the Vietcong.
   d. The marines then built a two-room schoolhouse for one hundred children.
   e. They set up a dispensary with a 200-patient capacity.

---

4. a. Eastwood Bleachwell lifts weights every day, trying to surpass his old records that he posts in his garage.
   b. He annually treks into the wilds of Baffin Island to hunt the wily white wolves.
   c. Bleachwell, the 38-year-old president of a large manufacturing firm, also thrives on water-skiing and body-surfing.
   d. Bleachwell's love of the rugged sporting life is shared by his beautiful wife Yvonne.
   e. He enjoys a hot game of tennis each day during a noon recess.

---

5. a. In a recent game against the Vikings, Melrose Lampwick ran the opening kickoff back for a touchdown.
   b. In the second quarter, Lampwick was tackled so hard by Dieter Schmidt, the Vikings' great linebacker, that he fumbled but recovered his own fumble.
   c. Just before the half, Lampwick caught a touchdown pass from Sandor Szabel to move Detroit ahead.
   d. On a quick opener, Lampwick ran fifty yards for a third-quarter score.
   e. Five minutes later, he iced the game for Detroit by kicking a 45-yard field goal against a stiff wind.

---

6. a. In Sinai's rugged desert, during the first day of fighting, Israeli tanks captured key towns and pocketed several garrisons of Arab soldiers in indefensible positions.
   b. On Wednesday, Israeli paratroopers landed near the Gulf of Aqaba to take Sharm el Sheikh and lift the blockade of the Gulf.
   c. In the second day of fighting the Israelis moved in one violent, lightning thrust to seal off Egyptian escape routes out of the Sinai Peninsula and destroy great numbers of Arab tanks and armored vehicles.
   d. An Israeli ambulance was blown apart when a wounded Egyptian officer who had been taken aboard pulled the pin of a hidden grenade.
   e. Despite fierce resistance from Jordanian snipers, the Israelis moved foot by foot through the old town of Jerusalem on the last day of the war.

---

7. a. A recent nationwide survey indicates that horror films featuring ghouls and monsters continue to lead Westerns (the next most popular type of film) by a 15 percent margin in the overall public response.
   b. The first of the truly great "horror" stars was Lon Chaney, whose roles as the Hunchback of Notre Dame and the Phantom of the Opera made him known throughout the world.
   c. Hungarian Bela Lugosi played Count Dracula with such evil charm that at one time in the mid-'30's he was receiving as much fan mail as Rudolph Valentino had a decade before.
   d. American adults and children alike thrilled to Boris Karloff's great portrayal of Mary Shelley's Frankenstein monster.

---

8. a. Whitey Schultze, who has never strayed far outside the city limits of Kenosha, Wisconsin, always tells everybody at the "Sit 'n' Sip" that he fought in the Battle of the Bulge.
   b. Whitey once informed the local scout troop that he had been a consultant to President Truman in Washington during the 1948 campaign.
   c. Schultze claims credit for having helped rescue three mine workers at a cave-in south of Johnstown, Pennsylvania, in March 1939.
   d. He insists that he turned down a gangster role in Hollywood during the '30's in deference to George Raft, who eventually got the role.
   e. Whitey admits that at times he "stretches the truth just a jot—for the sake of color."

---

9. a. Miss Marnie Machree, counselor at Minnehaha Girls' Camp at Fern Lake, Michigan, likes to do the frug and Watusi at the local pub.
   b. Miss Machree, during her off-duty hours, wears her miniskirt and does some singing with a small, nonprofessional group.

c. She has all the recordings the Beatles and the Rolling Stones ever made, and she listens to them for hours.
d. In fact, she once met one of the Rolling Stones quite by chance at a sorority dance at Michigan State.
e. Miss Machree likes to play her guitar and sing folk songs.

---

10. a. In 1925, when General Billy Mitchell was convicted of insubordination by a U.S. Army court-martial, the only member of the board who dissented with the "guilty" verdict was General Douglas MacArthur.
b. Mitchell had incurred the wrath of powerful officers when he proved in an actual test that a battleship could be sunk by aerial bombing, and he rubbed it in by telling the press how little foresight the "old-line" brass had.
c. Just prior to his dramatic demonstration of air power, Mitchell had been quoted as saying, "The General Staff knows as much about the air as a hog does about skating."
d. The year before his court-martial, Mitchell had publicly predicted with uncanny accuracy the 1941 bombing of Pearl Harbor by the Japanese, who were ostensibly friendly toward us in the twenties.
e. Even after he quit the army to avoid being ejected, Mitchell barnstormed around the country speaking on behalf of air power and the need to be prepared.

EXERCISE 14: *Make a single complex sentence out of each of the following groups of sentences. Place what you think is the most significant or striking element of that group in the main clause of your complex sentence.*

Example: Larry Nugent is a man who believes strongly in the virtues of physical toughness. So Nugent parachuted into Lake Tahoe recently with a group of marines.

Revision: *Because* he believes so strongly in the virtues of physical toughness, Larry Nugent recently parachuted into Lake Tahoe with a group of marines.

1. Lee Evans is a national champion quarter-miler for San Jose State. He beat all the rest of the runners in the last lap of the mile relay. He began thirty yards behind them.

45

2. Holy man Nashpur Karamcheti collected five hundred rupees from a crowd. The crowd had gathered to see him walk upon the Ganges. A moment later, he sank to the bottom.

_____

_____

_____

3. Keith Moran goes on a one-week hunger strike. He goes on a one-week hunger strike whenever he has an argument with his wife. His wife is a tyrannical woman.

_____

_____

_____

4. Clarence Darrow was a famous lawyer. Clarence Darrow didn't believe that teaching Darwin's theory of evolution to American youth would corrupt them. He defended teacher John Scopes of charges of "godlessness" in the famous "Monkey Trial" of the twenties.

_____

_____

_____

5. Everyone warned Guy Fawkes that blowing up Parliament could be dangerous. They said it could go hard on him if he were caught. Guy Fawkes tried it anyway.

_____

_____

_____

EXERCISE 15: *The object of this exercise is to compress all the short sentences in each of the following paragraphs into one long compound-complex sentence. The main clause of your revised sentence should relate to the topic sentence.*

Example

T. S.:   Skiing can be a hazardous sport.

Original: Fred Pebble is from Long Beach. He went skiing at Lake Arrowhead. Lake Arrowhead is in the San Bernardino Mountains. Pebble
broke his left ankle. Pebble tried a dangerous slope. Pebble is a
lawyer.

Revision: Long Beach lawyer <u>Fred Pebble</u> <u>broke his left ankle</u> when he tried
a dangerous ski slope at Lake Arrowhead in the San Bernardino
Mountains.

1. T. S.:   Great athletes often succeed in spite of their handicaps.

   Original: Jesse Owens' legs were injured. His legs were severely injured.
Owens' legs were injured in a childhood accident. He won
four gold medals. He won them at the Olympics. The Olympics
were held in Berlin in 1936.

Revision: _____

_____

_____

_____

2. T. S.:   Elmo Whipple finally went too far with the foreman.

   Original: Elmo Whipple has herded cattle for Alf Hanson for twenty-five
years. Whipple told Hanson's foreman Grubb Phillips that
Phillips didn't know a steer from a musk ox. Whipple was fired.

Revision: _____

_____

_____

_____

3. T. S.:   The local elementary school punished nonconformity recently.

   Original: Dolores Haze is a sixth-grader. She attends La Lolita Elementary
School. She was expelled from school. Her expulsion took place
yesterday. She was expelled for wearing a miniskirt and fishnet
stockings. This garb violated the dress code.

Revision: _____

_____

_____

_____

4. T. S.:   The state finally ended the disturbance caused by motorcycle gangs.

Original: One gang call themselves the "Filthy Few." They terrorized the town of El Burrito. El Burrito is in New Mexico. The New Mexico highway patrol surrounded them in a saloon. The highway patrol took them into custody.

Revision: _____

_____

_____

_____

5. T. S.:   A new weather prophet worked southern California doctors overtime last weekend.

Original: Emma Lavinia Hopewell is spiritual leader of a religious group. They call themselves the Children of the Flame. Thirty-seven members were hospitalized for sunstroke recently. They had stood in the desert for seven hours waiting for their leader to bring rain.

Revision: _____

_____

_____

_____

6. T. S.:   The town critic finally earned himself some grief last month.

Original: Pop Higgins never misses a chance to criticize the civic leaders. Pop publicly characterized the mayor of Middletown as being "several bricks short of a full load." The mayor is Art Primrose. Primrose sued Pop for slander.

Revision: _____

_____

_____

_____

7. T. S.:   In a novel by Joseph Conrad, the character Charles Marlow represents common sense and sanity in a chaotic world.

Original: Charles Marlow is a sea captain. In the novel *Heart of Darkness*, he patches up the pipes of his leaky old steamboat. He does this so that the steamboat can continue its trip. The steamboat is making a rescue trip up the river. It's the Congo River. Everyone else aboard the steamboat is running about in confusion.

Revision: _____

_____

_____

_____

8. T. S.:　Benvenuto Cellini is an example of the artist with destructive tendencies.
Original:　Benvenuto Cellini was a fifteenth-century Italian. He was a Florentine. He was a sculptor. He was also a lover. He killed more than ten opponents in rapier duels. He left us one of the world's most famous autobiographies.

Revision: _____

_____

_____

_____

9. T. S.:　Certain U.S. car manufacturers are learning a lesson from VW.
Original:　The Rambler American is made by American Motors. The Rambler American is the compact of the Rambler series. The American Motors Corporation has decided to abandon the annual restyling of the Rambler American. They intend to follow this plan for a number of years. By this means they hope to increase their sales. They hope to appeal to a conservative market.

Revision: _____

_____

_____

_____

EXERCISE 16:　*Do exactly as you did in the preceding exercise.*

1. T. S.:　Judging from recent transactions it would seem that artists aren't always poor.

Original: Andrew Wyeth is fifty-one years old. He is from Chadds Ford, Pennsylvania. He recently sold a painting. It was entitled "Her Room." It was sold for sixty-five thousand dollars. This establishes a record for an American artist during his own lifetime.

Revision: _____

_____

_____

_____

2. T. S.: The underworld becomes more ingenious every year.
   Original: A group of thieves discovered some rare gems in the Egyptian Museum. They discovered the gems last month. The gems were valued at five thousand dollars. The thieves got the gems out of the museum by washing them down a drainage pipe in the washroom and catching them in a screen about a mile from the scene.

Revision: _____

_____

_____

_____

3. T. S.: The nation's most publicized romancers are discreet about their plans.
   Original: Jet-setters Lavonia Nemwitz and Cesar Barranca faced the press in Acapulco, Mexico. Lavonia is twenty-two years old. Barranca is twenty-seven years old. They denied rumors that they were going to be married. They claimed they were merely spending a vacation in Acapulco, Mexico.

Revision: _____

_____

_____

_____

4. T. S.: Pablo Casals is noted for his sincere religious devotion.
   Original: The Archbishop of San Juan, Puerto Rico, said a special mass for Pablo Casals. Casals is a famous cello player. Casals was celebrating his ninetieth birthday. The musician wept as the mass was offered.

Revision: _____

_____

_____

_____

5. T. S.:   For some students, English composition can be a serious disap-
pointment.
   Original: Lazlo Tibor worked at least four hours a night on English. Tibor
is from Hungary. Tibor failed English 1A for the second time. He
received special help from the instructor.

   Revision: _____

_____

_____

_____

6. T. S.:   Lumir Zampach is a master of trickery.
   Original: Lumir Zampach is an American agent of Czech descent. He once
fooled the Russian train guards. It was on a train traveling through
Czechoslovakia. Zampach dressed himself as a conductor.

   Revision: _____

_____

_____

_____

7. T. S.:   Some professors' teaching philosophy stresses student discipline.
   Original: Martin Bratwurst teaches economics at Heidelberg University. He
once told a student that five hours of outside study was required
for every hour spent in class. Bratwurst said that the student's
absolute commitment to the subject was to be taken for granted.

   Revision: _____

_____

_____

_____

8. **T. S.:** Cecilia Selkirke prides herself on her faithfulness to her husband.
   Original: Cecilia Selkirke is a secretary for the Cooper Copper Company. She is a striking woman. Her boss, an affectionate man, repeatedly asks her to sit on his lap. She adamantly refuses because she is married.

   Revision: _____

   _____

   _____

   _____

9. **T. S.:** College students often stand up for their principles in vain.
   Original: Michael Monmouth attends El Borracho State College. Michael Monmouth is a sophomore. Michael is nineteen years old. He staged a five-day fast to protest the Governor's cutbacks in educational appropriations. He received no publicity for the protest. His fraternity forgot to inform the press.

   Revision: _____

   _____

   _____

   _____

10. **T. S.:** Actions speak louder than words.
    Original: George Bilkwood is a corporation executive. George lives next door to me. He has been claiming for years that he's a better singer than Frank Sinatra. He failed to make the choir at the Presbyterian church.

    Revision: _____

    _____

    _____

    _____

EXERCISE 17: *Read the following paragraph for unity. After deciding what the main idea of the topic sentence is, check the main clause of each subsequent sentence against that controlling idea. If you find sentences that are not directly related, try rewriting them so that they are subordinated to the main idea of the paragraph. Use your own paper for this exercise.*

(1) Judging from his performance in the past seven fights, Gregorio Panatela strikes boxing experts and fans alike as being the world's most effective welter-weight. (2) In March of 1965, Panatela went to Chicago to fight fourth-ranked Delbert Brooks. (3) He knocked out Brooks with a left hook in the final minute of the seventh round to earn a place in the top ten welterweights. (4) Three weeks later, Panatela went to New Orleans for a ten-round bout. (5) There he fought with an injured left hand, although he decisioned number one contender Artie Ponchatrain at the Municipal Stadium. (6) Panatela waited four months before flying to Lima to fight Peruvian welterweight champion Bartolo Ledesma. (7) He knocked out Ledesma at the beginning of the seventh round. (8) Last month he was in New York to face world champion Harvey Bromo in a nontitle ten-rounder at Madison Square Garden. (9) Panatela won a clear-cut decision after staggering Bromo twice. (10) He staggered the champion in the second round and again at the beginning of the ninth. (11) These victories over the short span of one year have earned Gregorio Panatela the title "The Uncrowned Welterweight King."

EXERCISE 18: *Do exactly as you did in the preceding exercise.*

(1) During Hitler's 1938 inspection of Italy's assets, Mussolini practiced his famous gift for creating the grand illusion. (2) Hitler's party was taken in a motorcade through certain streets. (3) These streets had been redesigned to look like movie sets. (4) Hitler viewed only pleasant, clean little Italian com-munities. (5) He didn't know that just behind the façade lay staggering squalor. (6) Hitler had traveled by train from Brenner to Rome. (7) Houses all along the line had been patched up and given fresh coats of paint. (8) It gave the illusion of a clean, thriving Italy. (9) Shortly afterwards, Hitler reviewed the vaunted Italian army. (10) The troops he reviewed were tall, blue-eyed, Aryan-looking men. (11) They had been specially chosen to lend the impression that Italians, like Germans, were Aryans. (12) Although the same men had been shifted from one spot to another ahead of the Fuhrer, Hitler thought he was reviewing dif-ferent men. (13) All this was to lend the illusion of great numbers. (14) Mussolini's misrepresentation of Italian grandeur ultimately may have helped defeat the Axis.

EXERCISE 19: *Do exactly as you did in the preceding exercise.*

(1) Eager to succeed in college, Matt Dillon experienced varied disappointments during his first four weeks at Cerebros. (2) All the first week he faithfully at-tended the lectures on composition, even though he failed to understand the explanation of topic sentences and found the concept of unity completely baf-fling. (3) During the third week he went to the library Wednesday evening to study Gibbon's *Decline and Fall of the Roman Empire*. (4) He got into an

intimate discussion with a brunette cheerleader, neglecting Gibbon and subsequently failing next morning's history quiz. (5) Then he thought he understood all his Chemistry 1A assignments. (6) However, by the end of the third week Mr. Allen suggested that he drop the course before the deadline. (7) On Thursday of the fourth week, in Miss McNeill's composition class, he composed what he would have sworn was a unified paragraph. (8) He was told the following Monday that due to a technical difficulty his paragraph did not count toward his grade.

3 Coherence

.

As we have been insisting, unity is a basic structural component of good writing. As such, it must be present in any piece of prose worth reading. However, unity alone—without the help of certain other qualities—cannot ensure a successful paragraph. Consider the following example:

> (1) Old man Suggins is the meanest man in Northfork. (2) He beats his wife once a week. (3) His kids always have bruises on their cheeks. (4) He burned down old Elmer Combines' outhouse because Elmer couldn't pay back a three-dollar poker debt. (5) Old man Suggins turpentined our dog Effie last May Day. (6) He said he had his reasons for doing it. (7) That's pretty rank, don't you believe?

Now this paragraph has unity, all right—all the facts relate to the idea that old man Suggins is the meanest man in Northfork. But in this case, unity alone fails to make the writing good. The prose remains choppy and abrupt. There is no relationship between individual sentences. It appears that the paragraph needs some words or phrases or signals that could ease the movement of the prose and make the separate facts stick together. This quality, which occurs when individual elements stick together, is called *coherence.* It's the companion of unity. It's the glue that joins the ideas together.

As you remember, unity dealt with the relationship between the topic sentence and each of the sentences that followed. Coherence involves the relationship that occurs from sentence to sentence within the paragraph. These sentences must flow together, must be woven together much as a fine piece of fabric must be smoothly knit. We don't expect to find snags, tears, and protruding threads in an expensive piece of cloth. By the same token, a good piece of prose should be free of awkward sentences and bumps in the "surface" of the writing. Consider the following student paragraph, which, in the quality of its content, is one cut above the preceding example:

> (1) It has become obvious that Senator F. Garth Doolin, III, is taking advantage of political position for personal gain. (2) One transgression was the taking of thirty-three trips on tax money. (3) Many Senate members had questioned the need for a tour of Africa. (4) Doolin charged it to an expense account. (5) His ex-wife complained of not receiving her annual allotment; he admitted to endorsing the checks and placing them in the bank. (6) Doolin has acquired a certain notoriety in the home district for having escaped payment of a twenty-five thousand dollar court order. (7) He has avoided it by going home only on Sundays. (8) The onlooker begins to wonder whether he can remain in office. (9) One typical voter put it this way, "Quit gripin', man. That guy Doolin's a swinger!"

The writer of this paragraph obviously knows what he's talking about. Its content, of course, is greatly superior to that of the opening paragraph on old Suggins. In the paragraph about Senator Doolin the writer has taken the trouble to get the facts, and he has unified these facts. But after all that good effort, he undermines the effectiveness of what should have been a fine paragraph. He allows his sentences to bump along in a staccato way when he could have smoothed out the writing with very little effort. He sacrifices ease in his writing by neglecting coherence. To avoid such pitfalls yourself, you can achieve coherence in any of a number of ways.

Transition

The readiest way of smoothing gaps in prose is through *transition,* a term that comes from the Latin *transire,* meaning to go over or across. Most people would probably agree that it's more pleasant to cross chasms on bridges than to try leaping over—much safer too. Like bridges, transitions open into two directions at the same time—forward to where the writer intends to go and backward to where he has been. Transitions most often are indicated by single words and short phrases, which can generally be positioned almost anywhere in a sentence. The following transitional words and phrases occur most frequently in writing:

To signal an addition:	and, furthermore, besides, next, moreover, in addition, again, also, similarly, too, finally, second, subsequently, last.
To signal an example or illustration:	for example, thus, for instance, that is, namely.
To signal a contrast or alternative:	but, or, nor, yet, still, however, nevertheless, on the contrary, on the other hand, conversely.
To signal a conclusion:	therefore, thus, then, in conclusion, consequently, as a result, in other words, accordingly, finally.

Let us see if the paragraph on F. Garth Doolin might be improved if we used some transitional phrases.

It has become obvious, *finally,* that Senator F. Garth Doolin, III, is taking advantage of political position for personal gains. One transgression, *for example,* was the taking of thirty-three trips on tax money. Many Senators have questioned the need for Doolin's tour of Africa. Doolin charged it to an expense account. When his ex-wife complained of not receiving her annual allotment, *moreover,* he admitted endorsing the checks and placing them in the bank. *Besides all this,* Doolin has acquired a certain notoriety in the home district for having escaped payment of a twenty-five thousand dollar court award. *Apparently,* he has avoided settlement by going home only on Sundays. *Consequently,* the onlooker begins to wonder whether this man can remain in office. *Yet* one typical voter may have voiced the sentiments of the district. "Quit gripin', man," he advised. "That guy Doolin's a swinger!"

Repetition

An equally important but much less obvious method of achieving coherence is through the repetition of and reference to key words in the paragraph. Often, these words are pronouns, but they may also be nouns and sometimes adjectives as well. For our purposes, nouns and pronouns are probably best. The student can no doubt see the reason why pronouns—words that are "stand-ins" for nouns—are particularly useful in linking ideas together from sentence to sentence. They establish a pattern of identity running through the paragraph by referring back to nouns or to other pronouns that preceded them. In their own modest way, these words keep the reader's attention focused continuously on the people, objects, or ideas that are the subject of the paragraph. Consider whether the coherence of our sample paragraph is further improved by the following repetition of key terms or substitutes for those key terms:

It has become obvious, finally, that Senator F. Garth Doolin, III, is taking advantage of *his* political position for personal gains. One transgression, for example, was *his* taking thirty-three trips on tax money. Many

Senators have questioned the need for Doolin's tour of Africa. Doolin charged *that venture* to *his* expense account. When *his* ex-wife complained of not receiving *her* annual allotment, moreover, *he* admitted to endorsing *her* checks *himself* and placing *them* in *his* Washington bank. Besides all this, Doolin has acquired a certain notoriety in *his* home district for having escaped payment of a twenty-five thousand dollar court award. Apparently, *he* has avoided *that* settlement by going home only on Sundays. Consequently, the onlooker begins to wonder how *this man* can remain in office. Yet one *typical voter* last week may have voiced the sentiments of the district. "Quit gripin', man," *he* advised. "That guy Doolin's a swinger!"

Modification

Modification is another method of improving coherence in prose. To modify something means to change it in some important respect. The enthusiast who modifies a stock-car engine, for instance, alters the standard specifications of that engine, hopefully in such a way that it has more power and thus can produce greater speed. In modifying his prose, a writer tries to give it more power by adding details to individual sentences. Most often, these details enhance the *specific* quality of the writing by contributing pieces of information that the reader wants to know. But modification can also improve the quality of coherence by keeping the reader constantly informed about the specific nature of the subject. Modification answers such questions as *who, how, when, where, why,* and *under what circumstances.*

Modifiers actually come in all sorts of shapes and sizes. They can take the form of single words, such as adjectives or adverbs:

Adjective:	an *impressive* Congressman
Adverb:	a *vitally* important law
Adjective past participle:	a *forged* document

These modifiers tend to affect the power of the nouns they modify. The modifier in the first instance announces that the Senator is impressive rather than simply a run-of-the-mill politician. In the second example, *law* (a neutral enough noun) becomes both important and vital after modification. In the third example, the document becomes an illegal one.

Modification can also be accomplished through phrases. The three most common types of modifying phrases are shown below:

A. Past participial:
1. *Forged by the counterfeiters,* the check was soon revealed to be worthless.
2. The check *forged by the counterfeiters* was soon revealed to be worthless.

B. Present participial:

    1. *Printing checks to their hearts' content,* the counterfeiters tried to deal with every bank in town.

    2. The counterfeiters, *printing checks as rapidly as possible,* tried to deal with every bank in town.

C. Prepositional:

    1. *After wrecking their press,* the counterfeiters decided to skip town.

    2. The counterfeiters, *after ruining their plates,* decided to skip town.

    3. The counterfeiters decided to skip town *after running into some bad luck.*

Note that the modifying phrases used above provide information about the crime. That is, the phrases *modify* the original situation by telling *who* in example **A,** *how* in example **B,** and *when* in example **C.** Note also that all these modifiers can be used at several places in the sentence. But of the three types of phrases, the prepositional phrase is the most useful and versatile. It conveys a wide range of information without cluttering up the sentence.

> The counterfeiters printed the money (at their hideout) (in an old warehouse) (on Ruskin Street).

In the above example, the three successive prepositional phrases tell *where* the counterfeiters operated. In the following sentences, we will try to use prepositions to tell *when, how, where,* and *why:*

> *In November* the counterfeiters, *in order to buy Christmas gifts,* printed the "tens" *on a new press in their hideout on Ruskin Street.*

Let us look at our sample paragraph once more to determine if adding some modification will improve its coherence:

> It has become obvious, finally, that Senator F. Garth Doolin, III, is taking advantage of his political position for personal gain. One transgression, for example, was his taking thirty-three trips *to Caracas, Venezuela, from Washington* on tax money. Many Senators questioned the need for Doolin's tour of Africa. *Accompanied by a pretty secretary and a lady corporation lawyer,* Doolin charged that venture to his expense account. When his ex-wife complained of not receiving her annual allotment *of twenty thousand dollars,* moreover, he admitted to endorsing her checks and placing them in his Washington bank. Besides all this, Doolin has acquired a certain notoriety in his home district of Williamsport for having escaped payment of a twenty-five thousand dollar court award *to Mrs. Madeline Bragg for slander.* Apparently, he has avoided that settlement by going home only on Sundays, *at which time he enjoys immunity from the courts.*

In the light of all these revelations, the onlooker begins to wonder whether this man can remain in office. Yet one typical Williamsport voter may have voiced the sentiments of the district *concerning Doolin's behavior.* "Quit gripin', man," the voter advised. "That guy Doolin's a swinger!"

Notice how, in addition to improving coherence, the above modifications help flesh out the prose by contributing information. We learn such things as *where* those tax-supported trips were taken, *who* went along, *how much* the annual allotment amounted to, *why* the Senator was being sued and by *whom.*

Logical Order

Modification can also be put to special uses in the paragraph. One such use that should be important to the serious student of writing is the establishment of *logical order* in the paragraph. Logical order helps to keep writing coherent because it ties the ideas to a distinct structure: time, space, or cause and effect, to mention a few possibilities. Before we take leave of Senator Doolin and his problems, let's look for one last time at the paragraph; this time we will establish a *chronological* (time) *order* by using certain kinds of modifications:

It has become obvious, finally, that Senator F. Garth Doolin, III, is taking advantage of his political position for personal gain. One transgression, for example, was his taking thirty-three trips to Caracas, Venezuela, from Washington on tax money *during the current session. Earlier in the year,* many Senators questioned the need for Doolin's tour of Africa. Accompanied by a pretty secretary and a lady corporation lawyer, Doolin charged that venture to his expense account. *More recently,* when his ex-wife complained of not receiving her annual allotment of twenty thousand dollars, moreover, he admitted to endorsing her checks himself and placing them in his Washington bank. Besides all this, Doolin has acquired a certain notoriety in his home district of Williamsport for having escaped payment of a twenty-five thousand dollar court award to Mrs. Madeline Bragg for slander. Apparently, he has avoided that settlement, *over the past two years,* by going home only on Sundays, at which time he enjoys immunity from the courts. In the light of all these revelations, the onlooker begins to wonder whether the Senator can remain in office. Yet one typical Williamsport voter *last week* may have voiced the sentiments of the district concerning Doolin's *future.* "Quit gripin', man," the voter advised. "That guy Doolin's a swinger!"

You may be likely to object at this point that the paragraph is "overdone." Perhaps it is a bit ripe. But if there is exaggeration here, it is meant to illustrate those subtleties in writing that lie hidden within the texture of the prose. These modifications aren't supposed to stand out, since good writing doesn't call attention to itself but rather to the subject it treats. Yet the student must try deliberately to see how these devices work before he can employ them himself.

EXERCISE 20: *First read the following paragraph. Answer the multiple choice questions that are at the end of the selection. When required to fill in blanks within the paragraph, choose the appropriate answer from the list given in the multiple choice section.*

(1) Certain authorities on human behavior claim that the costumes people wear to parties provide subtle insights into their personalities. (2) San Francisco psychiatrist Dr. Francis J. Rigney, for instance, suggests that the most timid guests arrive costumed in a conventional manner through fear of self-expression. (3) This sort of person will attend a Halloween party as a ghost or will arrive at a pirate party safely disguised as Long John Silver, complete with peg leg. (4) Other, bolder guests may think they are creating a certain image when actually they are revealing aspects of themselves that they'd rather not admit existed. (5) The woman who arrives dressed as innocent Little Miss Muffet, _____ _____, may be expressing the desire to retreat from womanhood, while another woman who comes dressed as Rita Hayworth may actually be sexually repressed. (6) According to psychologists, the most uninhibited guests will deliberately and sometimes daringly express their true personality by a carefully planned disguise. (7) Such people might appear in the guise of a historical personage whom they admire and perhaps resemble in certain respects. (8) Very seldom will they dress as animals or criminals but will wear costumes that display a healthy degree of self-esteem. (9)_____ they also have the freedom of personality to wear costumes that reflect a humorous sense of themselves. (10)_____, they too, like all the others, accepted the invitation to attend a costume party.

1. In sentence 2, the expression "for instance" is an example of:
   a. subordination
   b. transition
   c. modification
   d. repetition
   e. logical order
2. Choose one of the following transitions that best fits the blank in sentence 5:
   a. of course
   b. next
   c. moreover
   d. for example
   e. nevertheless
3. Choose one of the following transitions that best fits the blank in sentence 9:
   a. subsequently
   b. lastly
   c. yet
   d. namely
   e. secondly

4. Choose one of the following transitions that best fits the blank in sentence 10:
   a. still
   b. conversely
   c. accordingly
   d. however
   e. after all
5. In sentence 10, the pronoun "they" refers back *ultimately* to which of the following antecedents?
   a. "they" in sentence 9
   b. the women discussed in sentence 5
   c. "such people" in sentence 7
   d. "uninhibited guests" in sentence 6
   e. "animals or criminals" in sentence 8
6. The phrase "This sort of person" in sentence 3 is an example of:
   a. transition
   b. modification
   c. repetition
   d. logical order
   e. subordination
7. The phrase "through fear of self-expression" in sentence 2 is an example of:
   a. transition
   b. modification
   c. repetition
   d. logical order
   e. subordination
8. Which of the following best describes the type of logical order employed in the paragraph?
   a. time
   b. space
   c. moving from most timid to least timid
   d. cause and effect
   e. moving from least timid to most timid
9. In sentence 6, the phrase "According to psychologists" is an example of which of the following?
   a. transition
   b. modification
   c. repetition
   d. logical order
   e. subordination
10. In sentence 7, the phrase "Such people" is an example of which of the following?
   a. transition
   b. modification
   c. repetition
   d. logical order
   e. subordination

EXERCISE 21: *Do exactly as you did in the preceding exercise.*

(1) Not many American success stories can match the 1925 rise to fame and fortune of Illinois' Harold (Red) Grange. (2) The big ballyhoo that characterized his senior year began following a November 2 game when Grange was carried two miles on the shoulders of his peers. (3) Later that autumn, Grange's campus admirers circulated a petition nominating the 22-year-old halfback for Congress of the United States. (4)_____did Grange lack opportunities to earn big money. (5)_____, he enjoyed the luxury of refusing a $40,000 contract which the New York Giants offered him for his services in just three late season pro games. (6) Ignoring the Giants completely, Grange _____ accepted an offer from Chicago, who paid him twelve thousand dollars just to put his name on paper and an additional thirty thousand dollars for his first day's work, a game to be played on December 6 in New York. (7) Even the movies wooed Red, for a company called the Arrow Picture Corporation, now extinct, signed him to a contract on December 7. (8) Socially speaking, the highlight of the year came the very next day when Harold (Red) Grange was presented to President Calvin Coolidge in Washington. (9)_____ despite all the hoopla of the football season, Grange's image before the public turned out to be—as always with images—a fleeting thing. (10) Just five short years after his season of fame, "The Galloping Ghost" was reported to be working for wages in a Hollywood night club.

1. The phrase "following a November 2 game" in sentence 2 is an example of:
   a. transition
   b. repetition
   c. modification
   d. subordination
   e. logical order
2. Which of the following transitions best fits the blank in sentence 4?
   a. and
   b. when
   c. then
   d. nor
   e. next
3. Which of the following transitions best fits the blank in sentence 5?
   a. then
   b. in fact
   c. next
   d. perhaps
   e. however
4. In sentence 6, the phrase "Ignoring the Giants completely" is an example of:
   a. transition
   b. repetition
   c. modification
   d. pronoun reference
   e. logical order

5. Which of the following transitions best fits the blank in sentence 6?
   a. therefore
   b. consequently
   c. yet
   d. in addition
   e. finally
6. The phrase "called the Arrow Picture Corporation" in sentence 7 is an example of:
   a. transition
   b. repetition
   c. modification
   d. subordination
   e. logical order
7. Which of the following transitions best fits the blank in sentence 9?
   a. now
   b. moreover
   c. consequently
   d. finally
   e. yet
8. "The Galloping Ghost" in sentence 10 is an example of:
   a. transition
   b. repetition
   c. modification
   d. subordination
   e. logical order
9. The phrase "the football season" in sentence 9 refers back to:
   a. "the year" in sentence 8
   b. "that autumn" in sentence 3
   c. "senior year" in sentence 2
   d. "1925" in sentence 1
   e. all the above
10. The logical order maintained in the paragraph might best be described as:
   a. space
   b. cause and effect
   c. time
   d. moving from least to most significant
   e. both c and d
   f. both a and b

EXERCISE 22: *Fill in the blanks with the transitional expression that is best suited to the meaning of the paragraph.*

1. Although the average Vietcong guerrilla is not physically impressive, he is one of the world's most effective soldiers. Part of this effectiveness arises

from his ingenuity and his ability to make good use of discarded, apparently useless materials. He has, _____, been known to convert worn-out auto tires and empty French perfume bottles into military equipment. His ruthlessness, _____, is a quality that his enemy fears. Unlike most military men, he has no scruples about terrorizing a populace and never hesitates to enforce his authority with torture.

_____ to these qualities, his vast endurance permits him to carry on his fight with a minimum of logistic support. _____, his American counterpart complains about hiking a mere fifteen miles.

_____ the Vietcong guerrilla thinks nothing of marching over fifty miles a day for weeks on end. And he is able to subsist for long periods of time without elaborate field kitchens, _____ he is accustomed to a sparse diet that would send most GI's to the hospital in a matter of days. Most important, _____, is the fact that his leaders are capable and cunning, able to utilize his military effectiveness to the fullest by conducting a war that takes advantage of his strength and the enemy's weakness.

2. U.S. intervention in Vietnam has not been totally destructive. In the August 20 issue of *Time* magazine, _____, there is an article telling how Colonel David Clements and his Marine battalion rebuilt a small village, Le May, in the Elephant Valley deep in Vietcong country. Although Colonel Clements and his battalion had to fight to take the village, once they occupied it, they set to work rebuilding. _____they rebuilt two blown-out bridges and reopened the roads. _____ the battalion set to work reopening a store that had been closed for five years, thus making available many necessary items the villagers had not had for several years. A two-room school was _____ built so that over one hundred pupils could attend. The new dispensary, which is manned by Marine and Navy doctors, treats over two hundred Vietnamese patients a day. Colonel Clements believes "Someone has to win this war; to do that, we have to win the people. We won a few around here."

3. Over the past eight months, several events have established Buck Shawnley as the most controversial student body president in the history of OCJ.

_____ Shawnley ran as a write-in candidate on a platform that opposed "city hall and the *status quo* on all issues, both great and small." _____, after he was elected, Shawnley began to scrap openly with the board of trustees and the administration over a college dress code, which, he claimed, "perpetuated adolescent dependency and aborted individuality." The new president _____ used the college radio station to publicly censure the local voters, who had defeated a bond issue designed to gain funds for independent seminars on "everything from zither-playing to quoit-tossing." _____ did Shawnley spare the press, who he claimed "went out of its way to establish long hair on young men as the mark of the deviant, the unestablished, the resentful, and the untrustworthy." With all the adverse publicity he has received, Shawnley _____ regards the time he has spent as president as "a productive and happy chapter of my life."

EXERCISE 23: *Fill in the blank with the transitional expression that best expresses the logical relationship between the sentences.*

1. Hartley was short and homely, with a beaklike nose and a receding hairline. He had a bad temper, and he never missed a chance to cruelly embarrass his dates. _____ most of the women in our high school class were dying to go out with him.
2. Evolution has gifted today's mammals with a high metabolic rate and with the capacity to maintain a constant body temperature. _____ mammals are not a prey to the temperature of their immediate surroundings and can escape from the overheating or chilling that forces reptiles into dormancy.
3. The high mammalian metabolic rate does not come without its price, _____ , for a heavy intake of food is constantly required to sustain it.
4. The human brain at birth is about 330 cubic centimeters in size, not much larger than a baby gorilla's brain. _____ by the time both gorilla and man are mature, the man's brain is at least twice as large as the gorilla's.
5. Sir Garth Bridgeport is a scholar and a member of the Royal Society for the Advancement of Science. He is a distinguished racing-car expert, having designed last year's winner of the *Mille Miglia.* _____ , he is a champion chess-player and a fine polo-player.
6. Anton Ristic spent ten years at forced labor in a Soviet mine just south of the Arctic Circle. It is understandable _____ that he should suffer frequent nightmares.
7. Everyone became pretty frustrated after the rain had continued without letup into the twenty-seventh day. But _____ toward noon of that day the sun appeared for the first time in nearly a month, and the rain stopped.
8. Frostley doesn't indulge in smoking, drinking, or gambling. _____ is it likely he'll ever succumb to those vices.
9. After twelve hours, the jury could come to no decision regarding Vito Soriano. _____ Judge Ripstitch called for a recess until the following day.
10. There is one man and one man alone who could possibly speak without interruption for that length of time, _____ , Fidel Castro.

EXERCISE 24: *Sometimes the sentences in a paragraph are "glued" together so well that even when their order is deliberately scrambled, as it is below, a reader can rearrange them as they were in the original paragraph. Indicate the correct order of the sentences on the blank below. Be ready to support your rearrangement on the basis of signals that you find working in the prose.*

1. (a) One of the most surprising results of Robert Chabreck's tagging study was the revelation of a strong homing urge and capability in the alligators he worked with. (b) Another was found back in its home lake four years after having been released in a place 12 miles away. (c) This may not seem impressive when compared with the long-distance homing of pigeons, but it is an extraordinary performance for a creature that normally stays within half a mile of its den. (d) One made a homing trip of eight miles in three weeks, from a point to which it had been transported in a closed box. (e) The guidance mechanisms used in its homing feats are wholly unknown.*

Correct order: _____

2. (a) What happened in Los Angeles in 1960 no longer matters. (b) Neither will he ever quite forget those subsequent lean days as John F. Kennedy's Vice President, when—as one White House source politely puts it today—"Bobby was not as considerate of him as his brother was." (c) What matters now is what Johnson believes to have happened, and it is his conviction that Kennedy acted impudently and without authority in an attempt to keep him off the ticket. (d) The tangled relationship between Robert Kennedy and Lyndon Johnson is always thorny, but it blossoms into fresh new controversy every presidential election year.†

Correct order: _____

3. (a) He enforces the laws with undeviating severity while the Duke masquerades as a lowly friar. (b) Through one of Shakespeare's wrong-girl-in-the-right-bed plots, Isabella preserves not only Claudio's life but her own honor. (c) It is a play about honor that is marked by the lack of it: the lovers are mostly lechers, and purity is mocked as pretense. (d) In a fury of purity, Angelo orders a young gentleman, Claudio, to be executed for fornication. (e) *Measure for Measure* is one of Shakespeare's sour comedies. (f) Suddenly his puritanical iciness melts into lust, and he offers Isabella her brother's life in exchange for her body. (g) Claudio's sister Isabella, a

*Adapted from "Alligators: Dragons in Distress," by Archie Carr, *National Geographic Magazine* (January 1967). Copyright the National Geographic Society, Washington, D.C.
†Adapted from "Robert Kennedy and the *What If Game*," by Douglas Kiker, *Atlantic* (October 1966). Copyright © 1966 by the Atlantic Monthly Company, Boston, Mass. 02116. Reprinted with permission.

novice in religious habit, pleads with Angelo to show mercy. (h) Concerned about the state of public morals, the Duke of Vienna selects Angelo, a man of seemingly flinty virtues, to take full power over the state.‡

Correct order: _____

EXERCISE 25: *Do exactly as you did in the preceding exercise.*

1. (a) In between are several other varieties, including the small car, the American compact, the standard family sedan, and the American luxury car. (b) At one extreme is the limousine, which may appear to be a half-block long. (c) Cars now come in a bewildering variety of sizes. (d) At the other extreme is a vest-pocket foreign car that sometimes gives the impression that it could be wound with a key.

Correct order: _____

2. (a) Others write in their revisions between the lines in the margins or in the blank spaces at the top or bottom of the page. (b) Different writers use different methods when they revise their work. (c) And yet others staple their insertions to the sheets containing their earlier versions. (d) Some careful writers retype their work completely every time that they revise it. (e) Still others are cut-and-paste experts; they physically cut out unwanted material and paste in little pieces of paper with new, added material.

Correct order: _____

3. (a) Perhaps some day he will have an electronic device that types out automatically what he says—when he says it. (b) Today man may write with a lead pencil, a mechanical pencil, a fountain pen, a ballpoint pen, or even a typewriter. (c) Throughout history man has used a wide variety of instruments for writing. (d) Medieval monks often employed a quill to draw inked lines on parchment, a specially processed leather made from sheepskin. (e) Some ancient peoples used a sharp pointed stylus to cut lines on layers of wet clay, which later dried into bricklike tablets.

Correct order: _____

4. (a) His first political appointment on the Solicitor General's staff for the fifth judicial district of Georgia brought his name to the attention of the local public. (b) Senator Johnson came into national prominence when President Johnson appointed him Special U.S. Ambassador to the Zanzibar independence ceremonies. (c) Senator LeRoy R. Johnson of Georgia, a

‡Adapted from "The Theater," *Time* (February 24, 1967). Courtesy of *Time;* copyright Time, Inc., 1967.

Negro, has enjoyed a steadily rising political career. (d) Good publicity and solid accomplishments brought Johnson to the state legislature in 1962, making him the first Negro Senator in Georgia in ninety-two years. (e) But it was not until he was selected by the Atlanta Chamber of Commerce as one of its five outstanding young men of the year that Johnson came into contention as a serious political candidate. (f) Johnson's experience as an Atlanta teacher gave him an opening into politics.

Correct order: _____

5. (a) Things really began to get desperate when Dean Gradgrind placed all "questionable" textbooks on a prohibited list subject to examination by a community board of elderly ladies. (b) The Dean then extended the Friday work day until 9:30 P.M. with the institution of Friday evening classes. (c) The clincher came when the Dean was named President for the coming year, upon which occasion he took the opportunity to dismiss seven "defiant" English instructors. (d) In just one short year as Dean of Instruction at Milkweed, Dr. Josiah Gradgrind has managed to alienate the entire faculty. (e) The situation worsened at mid-year, when the Dean refused to extend any support whatsoever to a literature instructor who was being attacked by an adult student for "stressing a foul word" in J. D. Salinger's *Catcher in the Rye*. (f) Dr. Gradgrind first instituted compulsory attendance at divisional meetings once a week in order to "insure a cohesive spirit in keeping with the impressive tradition of Milkweed College."

Correct order: _____

EXERCISE 26: *The words in each of the following lists can be grouped into separate categories on the basis of association. After you have set up different categories, try to establish a logical order for the words within each of the categories. Use your own paper for this exercise.*

1. Hannibal, afternoon, near, Alexander, morning, Napoleon, evening, far, Westmoreland, Sheridan, there, Custer, Patton, night, Pershing, here, Attila
2. brave, mayor, illness, prudent, citizen, pentagon, president, virus, cowardly, triangle, governor, rectangle, weakness, circle, convalescence, recovery
3. Buchanan, precipitancy, elation, Kennedy, procrastination, serenity, punctuality, Madison, Garfield, depression, morbidity, FDR, gladness, haste
4. excellence, affection, ineptitude, dislike, capability, tolerance, incompetence, love, mediocrity, passion
5. pope, priest, recruit, college president, lieutenant, dean, cardinal, instructor, bishop, colonel, department head, corporal, student, general, layman, chief-of-staff

EXERCISE 27: *This is an exercise to help you understand the use of repetition in a paragraph. Each of the underlined words is followed by a word or phrase that refers to it. Circle every word or phrase that refers to the underlined word, and draw a line connecting the word or phrase with its antecedent.*

(1) No matter how their name changes from country to country, most bohemians tend to favor eccentric forms of behavior. (2) In Madrid, for example, gamberros enjoy illicit parties at the homes of wealthy people who happen to be out of town at the time. (3) These strange guests may also borrow an absentee owner's car while they are "tenants" in his residence. (4) Vienna has its Halbstarke, wild youths who wear black leather jackets and who affect an air of boredom with anything organized society endorses and even with their own ideas. (5) Although they have been known to terrorize people on picnics and outings, Austrian beats are not considered particularly dangerous to the safety of others. (6) Across the Iron Curtain in Prague, the hooligans have embellished the Czech language with their wealth of novel profanity. (7) But more than just the language is abused up north in traditionally peaceful Stockholm, where raggaren tear up and down the city's streets on motorcycles, terrorizing the populace in a manner similar to that of American Hell's Angels. (8) Sweden's new bohemians also like to "drag" the Kungsgaten, a major thoroughfare, noisily displaying their machinery to an annoyed populace. (9) Vying with the *raggaren* for Stockholm's attention are the mascots, effeminate-looking young men who wear face powder and lipstick and who wave their hair. (10) In Italy, the zazzeroni are the "great unwashed," whose protest takes the form of a refusal to bathe or keep themselves tidy. (11) These modern Romans copy many of the more outrageous habits of their American counterparts, the hippies. (12) So wherever he lives and whatever he does, it appears that a beat by any other name remains essentially a version of the beat that we in America have come to call our own.

EXERCISE 28: *This paragraph shows how coherence is achieved through the use of devices that link one idea to another. Moving from sentence to sentence, analyze the devices used for achieving coherence in the following student paragraph. Be prepared to discuss your findings in class.*

(1) During the past decade alone, economic prosperity in British Columbia has been increasing tremendously. (2) For example, during the last seven years the pulp and paper industry has doubled its production, earning twenty million dollars last year. (3) It is estimated that by 1970, this industry, with its current stock booming incredibly, will have tripled its 1960 output. (4) In another kind of economic venture, two thousand prospectors crowded into British Columbia's mountains last year, staking out eighty thousand mining claims. (5) Besides the

speculation of various individuals, five major mines are now in the process of getting into production. (6) Furthermore, as far as other natural resources are concerned, one of the richest North American oil strikes in a decade has been recorded recently. (7) Consequently, oil and gas production has increased two-fold in the past two years as a result of these northern discoveries. (8) As a result of all this exploding economy, British Columbians' personal income rose sharply in 1966, while capital investment, partly from the United States, climbed more than 16 percent above the level of the year before. (9) Judging from these statistics, one might do worse than to consider investing some capital in booming British Columbia.

4 Support

You probably recall our promise to discuss the subject of support in writing. Good writing must have concrete support just as a bank must have sufficient capital. After all, facts, ideas, and illustrations are the writer's stock in trade, the coin he works with. Without authentic material to back it up, writing has no value. Much student writing is, in fact, a declaration of bankruptcy. The following student paragraph, despite a certain unity and coherence, has no real content. There is no money in this bank:

> (1) For a beginning freshman, college is no easy thing. (2) It's very difficult, especially after high school, where you weren't given much responsibility. (3) Everything was cut and dried, and you had to do it. (4) But in college nobody forces you to do anything. (5) You just wake up one day and know you flunked. (6) That's what is so hard about college—having to do it on your own. (7) Nobody likes to have to suddenly shift for themselves. (8) Moreover, it's difficult to develop responsibility after being taken care of all your life by parents and teachers, and responsibility is a long process. (9) This is why college is tough for freshmen. (10) I know, because I flunked out after the first semester.

It should be obvious to you that if this student doesn't put some *content* into his writing, he is probably heading for a repeat performance of his first semester.

To stay in business as a college student, then, you must take the trouble to get the facts. No one is interested in reading a series of generalizations; it's too hard for the reader to relate them to his own life, to his own situation in the world. Writing takes on interest for the reader as it becomes *concrete*. Consider, for example, the fables of the Greek writer Aesop. Each one points up a moral or a bit of wisdom through a story. You'll recall that in the story of the town mouse and the country mouse, two rodents travel to the home of the town mouse in search of a more luxurious way of life. But when they sit down to the leavings of a penthouse feast, they are frightened away by the dogs of the house. The tale ends with a message: better beans and bacon in peace than cakes and ale in fear.

The wisdom of Aesop's judgment about life is driven home by the *specifics,* by the details of the story itself. No one would be particularly happy to hear the moral repeated over and over again without the story. Your writing, like Aesop's, must combine specific facts with generalizations. For the present, you should try to concentrate more on detail than on generalization in your writing.

Specific Support

Perhaps the use of specific detail could best be illustrated by another paragraph about the freshman's academic problems:

> (1) For the new freshman, adjusting to the discipline that college study demands is no easy matter. (2) Most difficult, perhaps, is accepting increased responsibility for unsupervised work. (3) In our English 13 class, for instance, a day-to-day journal was assigned in the first week, and no more was said about it for a month. (4) Suddenly, in the fifth week, Mr. Brimstone called for the completed journals, penalizing all students whose journals were incomplete. (5) One must also face the necessity of studying long hours outside of class. (6) As early as the opening Monday, the orientation instructor pointed out that in many classes at least two hours of outside study were required for every hour spent in class, and this turned out to be a conservative estimate. (7) I found, for example, that it took me an entire weekend to read even a book as interesting as John Steinbeck's *The Grapes of Wrath.* (8) The student must also face such minor problems as meeting only twice a week instead of every day, as in high school. (9) In such a case, the student sometimes tends to get "cold" in the four-day period between Thursday and the following Tuesday. (10) It becomes clear to me that President Stonehenge was right when he said in the opening speech to the freshmen, "Shake hands with the person on your left and then on your right. By the end of this semester only one of them will still be here."

You will probably find the above paragraph more convincing than the first one cited in this chapter. Undoubtedly, your increased interest results from the writer's use of specific content rather than generalizations. Notice the kind of facts or specifics that the writer uses. In sentence 3, for instance, we learn the specific name of the class, *English 13*—not "my English class" or, worse yet, "in one class." We find out in the same sentence that the assignment was made the *first week,* and in the following sentence we learn that the journals were called up in the *fifth week* by *Mr. Brimstone*—not just "the teacher." Sentence 6 contains several specifics: *opening Monday, two hours for every hour spent in class.* Sentence 7 contains the title of a book and the name of its author. Sentence 9 mentions the specific lapse of time occurring between classes. The concluding sentence contains an actual quotation—which is a very concrete type of support—and the name and position of the person making the statement. If you don't believe that it is the factual quality of the paragraph that improves the writing, consider what happens if we eliminate a few specific details. Let's leave out the quotation and the president's name:

> It becomes clear to me that our college president was right when he said that only one out of three of us freshmen would still be around by the end of the first full semester at this college.

How much less personal and dramatic this sentence becomes when the direct quotation and the speaker's name have been omitted! It's still factual to a degree, of course, but some of the life has been drained from it. An appropriate quotation, strategically placed, can add authentic detail and human interest to a piece of prose.

Perhaps at this point you think that most of what we're saying sounds all right in theory but that professional writers probably don't make a federal case out of using specifics. For the hardened cynic, the following paragraph might illustrate how an experienced professional *does* use details:

> (1) By January 31, 1967, the Secretary of Commerce—or, when a Transportation Department has been established, the Secretary of Transportation—will order that all new cars must meet the safety standards similar to those already issued by the GSA for government-purchased cars. (2) Most of these changes are not very dramatic: (3) some, such as outside rear-view mirrors, are items which formerly were "optionals" for the buyer; (4) some, such as padded dashboards, seat belts, collapsible steering columns, safety glass, dual brakes, windshield washers, are features which companies already had in effect, or say they had already planned to put into effect, for all cars. (5) Some, such as relocated knobs, head supports for front-seat passengers, padding for seat backs, rear window defoggers, and stronger fuel tanks, should be decided improvements. (6) All of these are expected to be in the 1968 cars. (7) By January 31, 1968, the Secretary will issue additional safety standards that, barring delays,

are to appear in the 1969 models. (8) The new standards must be reviewed and may be revised periodically.*

The writer of the above paragraph satisfied the reader's curiosity about those standards that the General Services Administration requires for government vehicles. When Mrs. Drew speaks in sentence 3 of *optionals,* she doesn't keep the reader guessing about what they are; she gives an example. When in sentence 4 she mentions *features which companies already had in effect, or say they had already planned to put into effect, for all cars,* she cites several of these specifically. In sentences 6 and 7, she mentions specific dates that are important to the subject under discussion. All in all, the use of details in Mrs. Drew's writing keeps the reader interested while it performs its major function—keeping the reader informed.

Biographical writing also benefits by the inclusion of detail. The following paragraph deals with Emperor Haile Selassie's exercise of personal power in Ethiopia:

> (1) Haile Selassie's beard may be flecked with grey, but his back is still straight and his command over Ethiopia as firm as ever. (2) He has put down three coup attempts in the past six years, for one of which four army officers are now on trial in Addis Ababa. (3) He is, in fact, as close to an absolute ruler as the century will allow. (4) Although he has permitted a Parliament to function for the past twelve years, he alone has the power to choose his Prime Minister. (5) He regularly plays *shum-shir*— the Ethiopian equivalent of musical chairs—to prevent his top ministers from gaining too much power, and he still serves as his nation's highest court. (6) Any subject in the land can appeal his grievances to the Emperor and get a personal hearing. (7) To maintain his authority, he employs a 35,000-man army, a 29,000-strong police force, and elite palace guard and three separate intelligence services.†

In the above paragraph the author frequently resorts to the use of numbers as a type of support in an age that loves statistics. The inclusion of the Ethiopian term *shum-shir* lends authenticity and a touch of local color to the writing. Once again, the writer has taken the trouble to be specific, and he has satisfied the reader's curiosity about Haile Selassie's rule over his subjects.

Sources for Specifics

Where does one find these concrete, specific details which we've said provide substance in a piece of writing? Actually, there is more in the world to write about than most people think there is. For instance, metropolitan newspapers

*"The Politics of Auto Safety," by Elizabeth Brenner Drew, *Atlantic* (October 1966). Copyright © 1966 by The Atlantic Monthly Company, Boston, Mass. 02116. Reprinted with permission.
†"Ethiopia: Lonely Emperor," *Time* (February 24, 1967). Courtesy of *Time.* Copyright Time, Inc., 1967.

are a daily and inexhaustible depository of facts. Clever students have even been known to use advertisements as a source of detail. Books, especially nonfiction, are often filled with the kinds of material adaptable to your paragraphs. Among nonfiction sources, biography and autobiography are especially rich in specific detail and have the added advantage of dealing with human nature, always an interesting subject. But as the paragraph on Haile Selassie suggests, perhaps the richest source of such information is a weekly news magazine such as *Time, Newsweek,* or *U.S. News and World Report.*

As a compilation of useful details, a weekly news magazine commends itself in several respects. For one thing, the information is current, and we're all interested in what is happening *now.* More significantly, it is highly factual in content, if sometimes biased in its selection of some facts and its omission of others, as we'll try to indicate in examples. Its most valuable feature, however, is its use of generally the same kind of paragraph structure that we've been advocating all through this book: strong topic sentences at the beginning supported by specific details and followed by a concluding or transitional sentence that usually summarizes the main idea of the paragraph and prepares us for the next. Few other publications inform us of current events while providing specific details to be used in our writing.

But how does one properly use the details published in a news magazine? Perhaps the best way to answer that question is to demonstrate step by step what one student did in constructing a paragraph out of facts he found in a *Newsweek* article. The following excerpt is from a *Newsweek* article entitled "Name Game: The Name."

As you read this article, try to surmise what *you* would do with it if you were asked to summarize it in one paragraph.

"Most of the names that you can think of today seem to be taken," says Walter Margulies of New York's Lippincott and Margulies, an industrial-design firm that has come up with such names as Montclair cigarettes for American Tobacco Co. and Citgo for Cities Service Oil Co. "And what makes finding a good one all the harder is that many of the new products that come out, like soaps and cigarettes and cars, are basically alike in function and appearance. So the name is sometimes the only real tangible difference between one brand and another. . . ."

The search for the right name is growing so desperate that some companies are abandoning individual brand names and bringing their products to market identified by the corporate surname (3M duplicating machines instead of Thermo-Fax). In a determined search for all the available alternatives, many others are turning to the computer.

Coca-Cola Co. found Tab, the name for its low-calorie soft drink, by computer, and du Pont plucked Corfam, the name of its new synthetic leather, from a list of 153,000 choices disgorged by a machine. Even Citgo, Cities Service Oil Co's new brand name, came from a computer.

Lippincott and Margulies counseled a Cities Service name change partly because surveys showed that many motorists thought the company was some kind of an urban public utility that only dabbled in the service-station business. The company didn't want to forsake its public identity completely so L & M decided to seek a word that began with "CI," the first two letters in its existing name. A computer thus was programed to produce the most promising combinations of four, five and six letter words that began with "CI." To avoid pronunciation problems, the computer was instructed to skip the letters J, Q, X and Z and any four or five letter combinations in which a vowel immediately followed the "CI."

Out came 448 four-letter combinations (including Cilk, Cine and Cico), 3,648 five-letter groups (Cissy, Cirly and Cisgo), and 76,800 six-letter combinations (Cibkib, Cikbyg and Citroc). In the end, after L & M researchers spent months weeding out the obvious misfits, they focused down to two finalists: Citco and Citgo. And Citgo won out, Margulies reports, because "it had more movement and sense of action." It cost Cities Service $20 million to change its name on everything from oil-can labels to filling-station signs, but the average cost of a corporate name switch, says L & M, is $300,000.

About the only kind of product a computer hasn't been asked to name yet is a computer. When RCA had to come up with a name for its new computer family, it used people—sixteen members of its corporate staff, who had a series of brain-storming sessions that produced such candidates as Cosmos, Realcom and Pan Data. They finally chose Spectra 70— Spectra to reflect its spectrum of power and applications, and 70 to imply that the machine will match any computer built until the 1970's.

In dreaming up their names, it is the fondest hope of every company that the public eventually will embrace their choice as practically a household word. But it is the supreme paradox of the name game that if a product is absorbed into the nation's vocabulary, it can become an everyday, lower-case generic word. And if that happens, competitors can legally jump in and start using the name, too. Many big companies—such as Coca-Cola and General Electric—maintain platoons of lawyers whose sole assignment is to protect product names [and] see that they are always upper-cased. If they aren't careful, they, too, will lose their hard-won brand names—just as Bayer Co. lost the exclusive right to aspirin, du Pont to cellophane and B. F. Goodrich to zipper.‡

The following paragraph was based on details taken from the *Newsweek* excerpt:

(1) *Newsweek* reports that the human mind has lately yielded to computers the process of devising appropriate brand names for products. (2) Recently, the Cities Service Oil Company relabeled its entire line of products "Citgo," a name chosen by an electronic machine. (3) Because the company wanted the new name to be somewhat similar to the old one, the computer was programed to produce more than eighty thousand words that began with the letters "CI," including such unusual combinations as "Cikbyg" and "Cissy." (4) Of the words the computer presented, "Citgo" was chosen because it suggested the motion appropriate to automobile accessories and

‡"Name Game: The Name," *Newsweek* (October 25, 1965). Copyright, Newsweek, Inc., October 1965.

lubricants. (5) Computers are naming not only entire lines of products but also individual items such as "Tab," a slim label for the low-calorie soft drink offered by the Coca-Cola Company. (6) This mechanized process is even creating names for single materials used in the make-up of products. (7) For instance, a computer produced the 153,000 possibilities from which the du Pont Company finally chose "Corfam" as the name suggestive of the new synthetic leather it represents. (8) However, computers have not been employed to choose the names for one important product: computers themselves.

Although the material in the *Newsweek* article may not have struck you as being especially promising, the writer of the above paragraph obviously was able to choose the details he wished to focus upon and to arrange those details into a meaningful working order. Let's trace the method he used to write his paragraph. He began by considering a number of possibilities for the main idea of the paragraph.

First possibility:	Focusing on the *process* by which the machine came up with the potential names.
Decision:	There seemed to be too little information on the process. Perhaps an account of the process could be incorporated in another way.
Second possibility:	Focusing on the *cost* involved in devising new names.
Decision:	Cost is mentioned in connection with only one product (Cities Service)—not enough information for a paragraph.
Third possibility:	Focusing on the companies that have used the computer process to find company names.
Decision:	This might lead to a simple listing of corporate names—all right for providing a few specifics, but not substantial for the main idea of a paragraph.
Fourth possibility:	Focusing on the *names themselves,* which all have an unusual sound and somehow suggest the product they represent.
Decision:	Perhaps this possibility could be combined with the *process* mentioned in the first possibility. The writer decided on this fourth alternative after a consideration of these possibilities.

Now let us examine the steps that the writer took in organizing the paragraph.

1. First he tried a tentative topic sentence:

   Computers are being used to think up appropriate brand names.

2. The writer defined the key phrase of the topic sentence as *appropriate brand names.*
3. The rest of the paragraph must support and develop that idea.

4. He must then find details to illustrate the controlling idea of the paragraph—the name must fit the product:
   a. "Citgo" suggests motion.
   b. "Tab" is terse and slim and suggests low calories.
   c. "Corfam"—probably a sort of poly-synthetic foam—sounds as though it should describe a type of leather.
5. The writer knows that in order to make the paragraph full he must do more than simply list the three names. He decides to include a general comment about the process of devising appropriate names by machines.

   The human mind has lately yielded to computers the process of devising appropriate brand names for products.

6. Notice: The writer has worked out a little theory of his *own*—machines are taking over typically human tasks. (Here's an instance of the writer trying an original approach but still using facts.)
7. By changing his tentative topic sentence slightly to the final, "*Newsweek* reports that the human mind has lately yielded to computers the process of devising appropriate brand names for products," the writer broadened the main idea to include a description of the process itself.
8. After a brief description illustrating the process used to produce Citgo, the writer moves through the other appropriate names in fairly quick order.
9. He chooses an appropriate ending—one that relates to the topic sentence but is not simply a repetition of the topic sentence. Actually, his conclusion is a clever takeoff on the topic sentence. He implies that "Computers have left to the human mind the task of devising names for computers."

In the construction of this student paragraph, the writer has made a generalization from a group of specific details. Then he has turned around and supported the generalization with those details. Note that the paragraph does not have the strict main clause unity we stressed so much before. Yet it does not sacrifice a singleness of purpose. By this point in the course, your instructor might be willing to give you the responsibility of maintaining unity without requiring you to make each main clause agree with the controlling idea, just so long as your paragraphs—like the one above—demonstrate a clear singleness of purpose. Perhaps you could also find your own approach to the facts you are interpreting. The above writer seems to suggest, without screaming about it, that machines are taking over in some areas. And he suggests it without altering the facts.

Separating Fact from Opinion

By this time we have harped so much upon the value of factual, specific support (as opposed to a generalization) that we've surely become bores. Try to fight off your fatigue as we attempt to make a final, clear distinction between a fact (sometimes called a "report") and an opinion (sometimes called a "judgment" or "inference"). Check the differences between the following sets of facts and opinions:

Opinion	Fact
Annette Spumoni is a lovely girl.	Annette Spumoni has an oval face, even features, blue eyes with heavy lashes, a brilliant smile, a rosy complexion, and shiny black hair.
Jason Wampum is a wealthy, powerful man.	Senator Jason Wampum's assets include a yacht valued at $150,000, two high-rise apartment buildings on Chicago's Lake Front, and a string of restaurants along the Pacific Coast.
By all the laws of chance, Japan's Pearl Harbor attack should never have succeeded.	In December 1941, the Japanese navy crossed the North Pacific at its stormiest season with a huge, conspicuous task force. It was spotted before the attack at least twice by civilian pilots. The force was also picked up by American radar but ignored.

As can be seen, facts are verifiable, objective statements based on measurement and observation. Any two of us looking at Annette Spumoni would probably agree that she has an oval face and blue eyes because we are members of a culture in which there is a consensus as to what shape *oval* describes and what shade constitutes the color blue. Regarding Annette's loveliness, however, observer A may disagree with observer B, since standards of loveliness tend to be a matter of individual taste. Thus, a *matter of fact* can be settled fairly impartially, but a *matter of opinion* often cannot, for an opinion is a judgment about an attitude toward a set of facts; hopefully, that opinion is based on facts. There are valid opinions and invalid ones. Do not assume from what we've been saying that facts are somehow more valuable than opinions. It is true that in a court of law, facts are generally required in proof or disproof of testimony. But opinion, especially if it is expert opinion from doctors or psychiatrists, is also valued when it can be established that the opinion is soundly based.

Needless to say, a good paragraph (in our opinion) has a high ratio of facts to generalizations. A generalization is made in the topic sentence and repeated in the primary support, which is discussed in the next chapter. But the secondary support—the real substance of the paragraph—is long on fact and short on opinion. Consider the following extract from *Newsweek*. We will then try to make a distinction between fact and opinion. Remember, we are recommending that you extract the *facts* from a magazine, not that you borrow its opinions or imitate the style or the wording. We don't want you to be guilty of copying from a book or magazine. However, facts are public property, once they have been published.

(1) Short, tubby Joseph E. Levine, at 60, looks like "the little king" of the comic pages. (2) But he is no laughing matter. (3) Producer, promoter, importer, showman, he is practically the last legendary-type tycoon of the movie business, and he lives and works in a properly baronial manner. (4) As a reaction from his sometimes shoeless boyhood, he owns vast quantities of Italian footgear—some 200 pairs by one estimate. (5) He has a 96-foot yacht in Florida and a nine-room, six-bath cooperative apartment in Manhattan lined with French impressionist paintings: Renoir, Vuillard, Monet, Degas. (6) Push a button, a screen drops from the ceiling, and Levine's luxurious living room is transformed into Levine's luxurious theater. (7) He can watch his movies: "Hercules," "The Carpetbaggers," "Two Women," "8½," "The Oscar" and "Darling" (for which Julie Christie has just won an Oscar) . . . .

(8) Today, as the king of the independents, Levine seems ready to challenge the majors. (9) There is talk about his becoming a public corporation. (10) At the moment he has 60 films in some degree of production, from "Nevada Smith," a spinoff of "The Carpetbaggers" that is about to be released, to "The Caper of the Golden Bulls," which will soon begin filming in Spain ("The star is . . . the star of 'The Oscar'," says Levine with Casey Stengel-like forgetfulness, "what's his name?").

(11) More and more Levine is branching out. (12) Now he not only buys films, he buys properties (such as "Generation," this season's Broadway hit with Henry Fonda) and even buys titles. (13) He paid Harold Robbins $1 million for "The Adventurers" before it was written, probably the highest price ever paid for a novel. (14) "As a businessman," says Levine, "it would have been foolish not to. . . ."

(15) Levine's power and money have earned him the usual crop of enemies. (16) "He has the most colossal ego I've ever encountered in the business," says one former associate. (17) "He spends money like crazy to show how big he is." (18) But Marcello Mastroianni says: "I think the best of him as long as he keeps producing my films. (19) His rashness appeals to me. (20) He's very simpatico." (21) "I've only known Levine for a short time," says prize-winning screenwriter Cesare Zavattini, "but I think it's possible to do good films with him—maybe because he thinks I'm a genius." §

Let's examine the factual content of the above writing and distinguish it from opinion. The numbers below refer to the sentences in the quoted selection.

1. . . . Joseph E. Levine looks like "the little king" of the comic pages.

   Opinion and generalization—the writer thinks so.

§"The Last of the Movie Barons," *Newsweek* (May 2, 1966). Copyright, Newsweek, Inc., May 1966.

2. But he is no laughing matter.

Again, opinion based on certain facts that we haven't learned yet.

3. Producer, promoter, importer, showman, he is practically the last legendary-type tycoon. . . .

Both fact (the first four modifiers) and opinion (Referring to him as a tycoon and describing the lavishness of his way of life both involve large doses of opinion).

4. As a reaction from his sometimes shoeless boyhood . . .

This may be a fact, but it would have stronger factual content if Levine had said it in a quotation.

. . . he owns vast quantities of Italian footgear . . .

A bit more specific, but still too general for our purposes—how big is "vast"?

. . . some 200 pairs . . .

Very factual, though only an approximate number. This is certainly a concrete detail.

5. He has a 96-foot yacht. . . .

Highly concrete and factual. Here is support for the early opinion "he is no laughing matter."

. . . in Florida . . .

Florida is a real place. That he anchors the yacht there is a fact.

. . . a nine-room, six-bath co-operative . . . in Manhattan lined with French impressionist paintings: Renoir, Vuillard, Monet, Degas.

This seems highly factual and specific. We have no reason to doubt that Levine possesses these things.

6. Push a button . . . and Levine's luxurious living room is transformed into Levine's luxurious theater.

Luxurious is an opinion word. But the information that Levine's living room is equipped with certain features is fact.

7. He can watch his movies: "Hercules," "The Carpetbaggers," . . . "Darling" (for which Julie Christie has just won an Oscar). . . .

This is factual, especially the listing of the titles of the movies which Levine produced. It's also a fact that Julie Christie won the award for *Darling.*

The third paragraph has one opinion (the topic sentence, number 15), which is supported with quotations from celebrities of the movie world. Direct quotations are highly specific and concrete in nature. Even though what Marcello Mastroianni says reflects an opinion, *that he said it is a fact.* If Mastroianni has been quoted accurately, his assertion may be used as specific support for a generalization. Naming the speaker is also a specific device, as is the citing of films by their actual titles in paragraph 2. In paragraph 2, we find a high proportion of factual content: "60 films in some degree of production," "Nevada Smith," "The Caper of the Golden Bulls," and "filming in Spain." These are all factual details that you could use if you were writing a paragraph on Levine or even on film production.

Let's review the ways for establishing concreteness and factuality in a piece of writing. These devices include the use of the following:

1. Simple statistics concerning a person's possessions or the names of places he came from, lives in, or visits.
2. Names of persons responsible for a quotation made in an article or persons named in connection with (in this instance) a movie or a book.
3. The quotations these people actually make.
4. Titles of books (*The Adventurers*) or plays (*Generation*).
5. Titles of movies (*Hercules*).
6. Actual events from the various news media. (We must assume that the news medium is accurate in reporting these occurrences.)

Avoiding Plagiarism

A constant danger in using facts from any source is that you will plagiarize, which means copying verbatim or even paraphrasing *too closely* what is found in an original source. To avoid plagiarism, you might try these practical suggestions:

1. If you use a fact or facts from a source, name the source in your paragraph (or in a footnote if you are writing a heavily documented paper).
2. More importantly, reword the factual statement *in your own* vocabulary. Do not lift the factual statement in its exact wording from its source.
3. Avoid using the same descriptive words (adjectives and adverbs) that are found in the original text. Look out for words in any source that are emotionally loaded—*scrambled, thrust, blasted, cheated, hostile, brutal,* etc.
4. If possible, choose facts from several parts of an article, not just from one paragraph in the article.
5. Avoid restating the writer's major opinions. Develop your *own* opinions based on the facts.

Unless you can distinguish the factual element in a statement and then express that factual element in your own particular way, you will be guilty of plagiarizing. Let us look at the following news article, which a student used as the basis for a paragraph. After you have read the article and what the student has written, you will have a better understanding of what plagiarism is. Hopefully, this example will help you to avoid it in your own writing.

. . . The other war, however, is of a different kind. As in centuries past, it is a grueling, grinding war between foot soldiers. Often in Vietnam it can be a maddeningly frustrating business. Such was the case last week when thousands of U.S. paratroopers of the 173rd Airborne Brigade joined Australian units in a sweep through the guerrilla-infested area north of Saigon known as the "Iron Triangle." Authorized for the first time in months to use tear gas to flush the Viet Cong out of their underground lairs, the paratroopers found plenty of tunnels but netted not a single guerrilla.

Nor are the frustrations limited to large-scale actions. Even more risky are the smaller, day-to-day encounters with an enemy who knows every trick of the guerrilla trade and who must revert to them increasingly in the face of the rapidly growing U.S. troop buildup which reached 140,000 men last week with the arrival of 11,000 GI's of the First Infantry Division. It is mainly in these guerrilla actions that the U.S. continues to get bloodied. Some examples:

South of the U.S. Marine base at Da Nang, a patrol of thirteen leathernecks was ambushed by nearly 200 Viet Cong, some of whom wore live ducks on their heads for camouflage. Popping up from bunkers and sugarcane stalks, the guerrillas let loose with small-arms fire that killed or wounded ten marines.

At the Bien Hoa Airbase, 15 miles from Saigon, a patrol of six sleepy-eyed GI's of the First Infantry Division moved out early one morning to secure a section of the base's perimeter. Suddenly, an ambush team of nine Viet Cong set off a Chinese-made land mine. "It knocked me down and there was this tremendous volume of automatic-weapons fire," recalled Radioman Richard G. Bahler, 22, of Holyoke, Colorado. "I just happened to look around behind me and there was this VC running right for me. He had an automatic weapon and he was just spraying everywhere." Shot through the hand and bleeding from shrapnel wounds, Bahler nevertheless managed to kill the guerrilla. Moments later, he was rescued by another patrol. "I checked my lieutenant," said Bahler. "He felt cold and clammy. The others all looked dead, too." They were.

Using one of their favorite wiles, Viet Cong snipers earlier in the week lured a company of paratroopers from the 173rd Airborne to a hill in Zone D and then proceeded to chop it up with withering machine-gun fire. As the horrified U.S. Commander looked on helplessly, a hidden guerrilla gunner played a macabre game with a dead paratrooper by rolling his body over and over with bursts of machine-gun fire. Hours later, after a small area of jungle was cleared, Air Force helicopters landed and evacuated the decimated company.‖

Now let us consider a student paragraph based upon the preceding news account:

‖"B-52's and Live Ducks," *Newsweek* (October 18, 1965). Copyright, Newsweek, Inc., October 1965. [Underscores added.]

(1) The buildup of U.S. troops in Vietnam has caused the guerrillas to be very tricky. (2) The U.S. troop buildup has reached 140,000 men in the last week with the arrival of 11,000 G.I.'s of the First Infantry Division. (3) As a result of the U.S. troop buildup there has not been any large-scale action. (4) The guerrillas, which know every trick of guerrilla warfare, have been using snipers and small bands of men to ambush companies of scouting parties of U.S. soldiers. (5) An example of the sly trickery used by the guerrillas is the ambush of a U.S. company of paratroopers from the 173rd Airborne Division. (6) The company was lured to a hill in Zone D by snipers. (7) When the company reached the hill the guerrillas began to chop them down by withering machine-gun fire. (8) A U.S. commander looked on hopelessly as a guerrilla played macabre games with a paratrooper. (9) Later the area was cleared, and helicopters evacuated the decimated company.

Comparing the underlined portions of the above paragraph with the corresponding portions of the original article will reveal the extent of the student's plagiarism. Fortunately, after some consultation with the instructor, he was able to make more honest use of the same source of information. In the process of ridding his paragraph of the taint of plagiarism, he also tightened it up in its unity and coherence:

(1) Responding to the increase of U.S. troops to 140,000 last week, the Vietcong began resorting to some deadly jungle trickery, according to *Newsweek,* October 18, 1965. (2) Late in the week, the VC used small explosives to stop a patrol of six Americans on the outskirts of the airbase at Bien Hoa. (3) Radioman Richard Bahler, the only survivor of the conflict, related that the VC had begun the ambush by exploding a land mine that knocked down the men and made them an easy mark for rifle fire. (4) The enemy also resorted to wearing live ducks on their heads to stage a surprise for a marine patrol at Da Nang earlier in the week. (5) Jumping up suddenly from the sugar-cane thickets, 200 VC killed or wounded ten of the marines with small-arms fire. (6) At the start of the disastrous week, enemy snipers drew an entire paratrooper company from the 173rd Airborne up a hill in Zone D and annihilated them with machine guns. (7) So effective was the ambush that it took American helicopter rescue teams several hours to clear a patch of jungle to evacuate the few surviving Americans.

Unpleasant as the subject of the paragraph is, the writing is good, and the student avoids plagiarism while using the factual and specific content of the original source. Plagiarism *always* constitutes a problem for student papers of all kinds, for students are continually looking to outside sources for information. It isn't wrong to rely on what you read. You have a perfect right to increase your knowledge by resorting to outside sources for information, but in using that material in your writing you must find your own words and your own style.

Summary

1. Good writing is a combination of opinion and fact, but, practically speaking, more fact than opinion is desirable in most student writing.
2. Topic sentences convey an opinion that most of the remaining sentences support factually.
3. Specifics (concrete items) include such "things" as numbers, names, titles of works, statistics, quotations, and the narration of events that took place.
4. Useful sources of specific details include metropolitan newspapers, biographical and nonfictional works, news magazines, textbooks, and one's own observation of the environment.
5. Fact deals with what actually occurred or exists; opinion makes a judgment concerning that actual occurrence or state of being.
6. Cite your source somewhere in your paragraph.
7. Above all, any material that you use must be expressed *in your own terms* and not in the terms of a professional writer. Base your own opinions on the facts. Come to your own conclusions regarding the facts.

Facts are the *substance* of a piece of writing—the marks of its authenticity. You can't write convincingly unless you have something to write about. Maybe even old Aesop would agree with us when we conclude with a moral of our own:

You can't make chicken salad out of feathers.

EXERCISE 29: *In the blank preceding each of the following statements, indicate whether the statement is a fact or an opinion with the letters F or O.*

_____ 1. Americans are essentially an idealistic people who tend to take their democracy straight.

_____ 2. Despite the appearance of an occasionally sincere and just objector, the hippie movement is characterized by massive immaturity.

_____ 3. Near Agra in northern India, a man named Goonga charges onlookers five rupees in return for performing a 170-foot dive into a reservoir forty feet deep that is always at least half full of water.

_____ 4. The most formidable fighting man the world has ever known is the Apache Indian of the southwestern United States.

_____ 5. Performed regularly in Bangkok, Thai boxing allows the use of the feet as well as the fists and features the same weight divisions that are used in Western boxing.

_____ 6. Thai boxing tends to be much more rugged and dangerous than Western boxing.

_____ 7. Acupuncture and moxibustion, two ancient Chinese medical techniques going back twenty-five hundred years and still being practiced in Hong Kong, feature the application of needles to nerve ends at from three hundred to eight hundred points on the human body.

_____ 8. Based on philosophies of nature and religion, this ancient form of medicine could teach much to Western physicians.

_____ 9. In the New Guinea highlands, tribesmen of the Mogei are just beginning to emerge from the Stone Age and may never become civilized enough to warrant the privilege of self-government.

_____ 10. President Lyndon Baines Johnson has been characterized by writer James Deakin as "the Paul Bunyan of Presidents and the glowing embodiment of the American Dream [playing] center stage under a spotlight that rarely dims to applause that never stops, if he can help it."

EXERCISE 30: *Do exactly as you did in the preceding exercise.*

_____ 1. Ever since his rise to Presidential power, Lyndon Johnson's dealings with Washington's vast and influential press corps have been on touchy grounds.

_____ 2. Negro rioting during the hot months in major cities can only increase in years to come.

_____ 3. The second most costly and serious of the 1967 riots occurred in Newark, New Jersey, where over one thousand people were injured within a period of four days.

_____ 4. "Man has survived, hitherto, by virtue of ignorance and efficiency," Bertrand Russell has said. "He is a ferocious animal and there have always been powerful men who did all the harm they could."

_____ 5. The distance from Earth to the nearest fixed star has been computed at twenty-five million miles.

_____ 6. Says Arthur Schlesinger, Jr., "The common man has always regarded the great man with mixed feelings—resentment as well as admiration, hatred as well as love."

_____ 7. Man is a mere child in terms of the age of the world that surrounds him, and a day of unbelievable length extends before him.

_____ 8. The United States is a nation that has scarcely begun to recognize its potential for greatness and sovereignty.

_____ 9. The most dangerous land reptile in the world is the Australian tiger snake.

_____ 10. As little as 1/14,000 of an ounce of tiger snake venom (two milligrams) can cause swift death by lung paralysis.

EXERCISE 31: *In this exercise you are required to extract the facts from the following sentences and to create your own sentence from these facts. First, cross out any word or phrase that is not factual. It's permissible to add a neutral word if it's needed to make sense out of what remains.*

Example:

Original: Present on Al Sullivan's July 13 program were ~~beefy~~ Garson Caldwell, former Chicago Bear backfield great, and ~~muckraker~~ Ralph Nader, who last year ~~blew the whistle~~ on the automobile industry, charging Detroit with carelessness in installing safety devices.

Revision: On July 13, Al Sullivan's program featured Ralph Nader, who has recently accused the auto industry of being negligent over safety, and Garson Caldwell, who once played in the Chicago Bear backfield.

1. In a raging denunciation launched from the Beverly Hilton against "right-wing party policies," liberal Republican Congressman Richard Hanes blasted especially what he tagged "fear campaigns within the party" and "reactionary policies that advocate one step forward for every three steps back."

_____

_____

_____

2. In the Venetian Room of San Francisco's Fairmont Hotel last week, Wilma Peepgrass, plump and fiery Western States Secretary of the National Women's Temperance Union, bitterly lashed out against the national trend toward teenage tippling, calling it "a sickening descent into bestiality and drunkenness."

_____

_____

_____

3. Suave Turkish diplomat Ahmed Bey preferred to remain cool last week toward a U.S. pitch that the Dardanelles and the Bosporus be more heavily patrolled by allied forces in the eastern Mediterranean.

_____

_____

_____

4. "So far management has had the situation wired their way. But things will be different after the next election," snickered Coley Bilgewell, muscleman chief of local unions, at a raucous rally aimed at pumping up the assets of *The Timekeeper,* Bilgewell's union propaganda newspaper.

_____

_____

_____

5. According to the May 13, 1967, *New Republic,* "Smith, Kline & French Laboratories, the firm that makes all those Bennies and Dexies that millions of adult pillheads use, has joined the National Education Association in a book, *Drug Abuse: Escape to Nowhere,* that advises schoolteachers how to cooperate with the authorities in nabbing youthful potheads."

_____

_____

_____

EXERCISE 32: *Do exactly as you did in the preceding exercise.*

1. Paunchy, pinstriped Raymond "Muley" Sammins became the segregationist governor of Louisiana yesterday after a four-month campaign that recalled Huey Long's grass-roots pitch of the thirties.

_____

_____

2. In Garden Grove, racist H. Milford Meadows addressed 550 fellow rightists of the John Birch Society last night in an hour-long harangue against what at one point he slyly called "bleeding heart economic relief policies in the state."

_____

_____

_____

3. For thirty minutes, the defense attorney grilled J. D. Jackson, beefy, florid Muskaloosa County sheriff, whose corn-pone surface manner hides the brutality that allegedly caused county jail prisoners to scream about conditions to Governor Arkley J. Wright last May.

_____

_____

_____

4. Ever since he sang to the FBI about underworld affairs last January, mobster Tony (Big Pinkie) Pingitore has been holed up in southern Wisconsin trying to shake the racketeers who once made him wealthy and now want him hit.

_____

_____

_____

5. In Buenos Aires, Costa Rican man-about-town Jorge Alvarez tipped off the press today that he and American cineminx Loretta LaMesa were going to be married, a move that insiders claim is a way for playboy Jorge to stop alimony payments to his ex-wife, British cinema queen Elaine Bevan.

_____

_____

_____

EXERCISE 33:   *In this exercise you are asked to develop your own paragraph from the facts provided in the following short article. As you read it, surmise how you might organize a paragraph based on the facts about Count Luckner. Before you begin to write, however, answer the questions that follow this article. Make sure that you use your own words.*

The Sea Devil

Some say the last great pirate met his end when Edward Teach (Blackbeard to history) was killed in a Virginia river battle in 1718. Others contend that the Age of Piracy didn't close until freebooter Jean Lafitte disappeared into the Caribbean with his treasure in 1821. But to a generation of schoolboys now reaching middle age, the most magnificent marauder of the seas was Count Felix Luckner of Kaiser Wilhelm's Imperial Navy. . . .

Luckner—or the Sea Devil as he came to be called—was the very model of a modern buccaneer. He sailed under the German naval ensign instead of the Jolly Roger, and his prisoners succumbed to champagne and his courtly charm instead of to cutlasses. In seven months of 1917, his three-masted windjammer sent fourteen Allied ships to the bottom with a romantic flair that amused rather than terrorized the southern sea lanes and made Luckner into a postwar hero on both sides of the Atlantic.

His strongest weapons were the benign profile of his vessel and the theatrical talent of his crew. At the helm of a captured American clipper rechristened the *Seeadler* (Sea Eagle) and specially outfitted in Hamburg as a Norwegian cargo ship above decks but a German auxiliary cruiser below, Luckner would peacefully glide up to a French or British freighter signaling some innocuous nautical request like "Chronometer time, please." The captain would slow down, disarmed by the Norwegian flag at the *Seeadler*'s mast and the sight of a woman on deck (Scandinavian skippers often take their wives along on cruises, so Luckner assigned a boyish crew member to don wig and skirts when a victim was sighted). Then, with well-trained precision, German colors were run up, a section of the rail clattered down to reveal a single cannon, and signal flags broke out with the warning: "Heave to or I will fire."

After each capture, the stupefied enemy captain and crew were taken aboard the *Seeadler,* and their ship was quietly sunk. In most cases, however, it wasn't long before they could be counted among the war's most contented prisoners— or, as Luckner preferred to call them, "guests." The captured captain was escorted to a plush cabin in the "Captains' Club" where he joined the skippers of earlier catches. All prisoners had virtual run-of-the-ship, and French and British magazines and phonograph records had been laid in for their amusement. Luckner offered a prize of £10 and a bottle of champagne—he had acquired 2,300 cases of Veuve Cliquot from one of his prizes—to the first man to spot enemy ships, and soon even his "guests" were scrambling up the rigging to search the horizon.

Not a man was ever lost in any of the *Seeadler*'s engagements. When his guest quarters became packed with more than 400 Allied seamen, Luckner stopped a French barque bound for Brazil and put them aboard, gallantly paying them full wages for the time spent on his ship and toasting them with a final glass of champagne. Then he ducked around Cape Horn into the Pacific to elude the warships sure to be after him, sank a few American vessels south of Hawaii, and was finally wrecked by a tidal wave in the Society Islands. After 2,300 miles of island-hopping in an open boat, he was caught by the British in the Fiji Islands. He could have avoided capture by using force but disdained because he was not in uniform.

Luckner's early career matched his war exploits perfectly. He ran away from his aristocratic Dresden family when he was 13 and sailed as a cabin boy in a Russian full-rigger. Tumbling from one adventure to another around the world, he became a kangaroo hunter, beach-comber, Mexican soldier, prizefighter, wrestler, and a member of the Salvation Army. Finally he got a chance to study for a naval commission and was picked to command the *Seeadler* because no one else had his sailing experience.

Once the war was over, however, Luckner could never recapture the romance of his buccaneering days. On successive world tours he gave rousing accounts of his voyages and, in the '30s, tried some feeble propaganda for Hitler. In 1939, too old for active service and somewhat suspect by the Nazis, he retired to a hunting lodge in the Harz Mountains. But the old pirate's spirit never waned: in 1941 he wrote wistfully to his biographer Lowell Thomas, "My yacht *Sea Eagle* is berthed in Stettin waiting for new adventure."¶

1. List five or more adjectives that you think describe Luckner's character or exploits.

_____

_____

2. Choose the *one* adjective you think has the best possibility for development by facts found in the above article and define that adjective.

_____

_____

3. Make that adjective the controlling idea of one of the following topic sentences:
   During the First World War, Count Felix Luckner _____

_____

   Although buccaneers like Blackbeard and Henry Morgan established a

   tradition of violence, _____

_____

4. Select a list of specifics from the article that support your controlling idea. You might try composing a brief outline:

   T. S.: _____

       I. _____

           A. _____

           B. _____

     II. _____

           A. _____

           B. _____

¶ "The Sea Devil," *Newsweek* (April 25, 1966). Copyright, Newsweek, Inc., April 1966.

5. Using your fact sheet or outline, write a unified, coherent, factually supported paragraph of at least 130 words.

EXERCISE 34: *Read the article below and do the exercises that follow it.*

The Italians have a word for it—graffiti, the anonymous one-line scrawlings found on fences, billboards, sidewalks and washroom walls. Usually graffiti has ranked one rung below limericks on the literary scale, but lately the messages have gained a new respectability. Playwright Edward Albee admits that an inscription in a Greenwich Village lavatory inspired the title for his "Who's Afraid of Virginia Woolf?" After Yale University released a map indicating that the Vikings rather than Columbus discovered America, the *New York Times* chose a graffito from an Italian district in Boston for its quotation of the day: "Lief Ericson is a Fink." Even the scholars have taken note of the washroom wit. In a new study entitled "What the Walls Say Today," two UCLA professors suggest that graffiti may offer a message of sorts about human nature.

For five months, psychiatrist Harvel Lomas and his associate Gershen Weltman scoured Los Angeles's bars, restaurants, bus stations, schools and even hospitals. Their report, read at a recent meeting of the American Psychiatric Association, concluded that people write graffiti to prove themselves ("This Is Tony's Turf"), to insult ("Hugh Hefner Is a Virgin"), to excite others sexually ("Marion: $25"), and to communicate an opinion ("Marvin Can't Relate to His Environment") or a bit of humor ("Judge Crater—Please Call Your Office Immediately").

Although slum buildings and automobile underpasses yielded the most graffiti, the investigators claim that the urge to make one's mark is common to all classes. Among good, law-abiding middle-class types it is expressed through what Lomas and Weltman call "commercial graffiti"—bumper stickers and buttons. And if one is rich enough, says Lomas, he simply has his name inscribed over the lobby entrance of a 40-story building instead of painting it on a fence.

In passing, the researchers discovered that the legendary "Kilroy" is being challenged by a new, equally mystifying figure—"Overby." Usually, Overby graffiti announces little more than "Overby Lives" or "Overby Rules" or, as a sign off the Pacific Coast Highway put it, "Overby Has a Heskinny in His Frebus." At times, however, Overby seems to represent the unknown hand that picks young grafficionados for the Army; in Los Angeles one roadside sign read "Down with the Draft—Overby Strikes Every 7 Hours."

Judging from the graffiti around southern California beaches, the biggest teen-age hangups are psychedelics ("Take LSD and SEE") and the discovery that the world is not Disneyland ("Mary Poppins Is a Junkie"). . . . University of Chicago students have compiled an anthology of bromides from Western movies on a Lake Shore Drive underpass: "I Don't Need No Stinking Badge," "He's Not Dead—He's in the Hills—But He'll Be Back if We Need Him." Some of the most sophisticated graffiti appears on the walls of the men's room in Harvard's Lamont Library: "Reality Is a Crutch," "War Is Good Business—Invest Your Sons" and "God Isn't Dead—He Just Doesn't Want to Get Involved."

Public personalities, of course, draw a heavy share of wall commentary. The current favorites: "J. Edgar Hoover Sleeps with a Night Light"; "Stamp Out Bert Parks"; "Ad Hoc Committee to Draft George Hamilton"; "Ronald Reagan Eats Peanut Butter". . . .

Lately, more and more grafficionados seem to get their kicks from commenting on the works of others. On a New York subway poster, for instance, the message "Jesus Saves" has inspired the reply "But Moses Invests." A graffito in a San Francisco bar proclaims "My Mother Made Me a Homosexual"; beneath, someone has written "If I Buy Her the Wool, Will She Make Me One Too?" But the last word in dialogues appears on the washroom wall in New York's White Horse Inn. Writer A has written "I Love Grils." Writer B has crossed this out and corrected, "It's Girls, Stupid—G-I-R-L-S." Under which Writer C has scrawled "What About Us Grils?"**

1. In the article above, what seems to be the main idea?

_____

_____

_____

2. At what point in the article is this idea most obviously stated? State it in your own terms:

_____

_____

_____

3. In the second paragraph, the writer classifies the major reasons people write graffiti according to recent research findings. Can you find some graffiti somewhere that indicate still *other* motives? Write a paragraph classifying the graffiti you find.

4. Can you also apply the author's main idea to buttons or to bumper stickers? What do the buttons or bumpers say to you? Write a paragraph giving the reasons why people display the particular stickers that they do. What does the sticker say about the person who owns it? See the following lists:

Bumper Stickers

No Tuition	If You Can Read This,
Support Your Local Police	You're Following Too Close
Vote No for Governor	Nix Nixon
Impeach Earl Warren	Make Love, Not War

**"Washroom Wit," *Newsweek* (October 10, 1966). Copyright, Newsweek, Inc., October 1966.

Mary Poppins Is a Junkie
Parking Problems? Support
   Planned Parenthood
No on 14
Help Stamp out Literacy—
   Vote Yes on Tuition
Your Local Policeman Is Armed
   and Dangerous
Support Mental Hygiene or
   I'll Kill You
God Is Alive and Lives in the
   White House
AuH_2O-64
Impeach Bonzo and His Co-Star
KSFO Loves You

Help Stamp Out Bumper Stickers
Hitler Lives!
Get U.S. Out of U.N.
I Support the War on Poverty—
   I Work
Our Position—No Tuition
Repeat Inhibition
Old Enough to Fight, Old
   Enough to Vote
Peanut Butter Is Better than Pot
Love Is Lovely, War Is Ugly
Curse You Red Baron
War Is Good Business—Invest
   Your Son

Buttons

Bring Back Paganism
Socrates Eats Hemlock
Save Water: Shower with a Friend
Keep the Faith, Baby
Sex Before Finals
Batman Loves Robin
I Am a Human Being: Do Not Fold,
   Spindle, or Mutilate

Mozart Forever
Apple Pie Can Make You Sterile
Marcel Proust Is a Yenta
Ban Buttons
If It Feels Good I'll Do It
Draft Beer Not Students
I Like Older Women
Dr. Spock Wears Rubber Pants

5. This article was written in 1966. Can you compile a list of new and different graffiti that you have observed? Classify these according to topic. Write
a paragraph of your own accounting for these graffiti. Try a simple outline.
(See Chapter Five for outline form and procedure.)

T. S.:
   I.
      A.
      B.

6. The fifth paragraph classifies the subjects of teenage graffiti. Make your
own set of classifications into which you place the graffiti that you have
discovered.

EXERCISE 35: *Use the following fact sheet as the basis for a paragraph or a
short essay. You need not use all the facts. It may help you
in organizing the paragraph if you divide the facts into suitable
categories. Label the categories accordingly. Use your own
paper for this exercise.*

1. Twiggy is a British fashion model.
2. She is a teen-ager.
3. She is five feet six inches tall.
4. She weighs ninety-one pounds.
5. Her real name is Lesley Hornby.
6. She comes from London.
7. Twiggy has taken over fellow Britisher Jean Shrimpton's position as the world's most publicized fashion model.
8. Says Su Dalgleish, a newspaper fashion writer, "With that underdeveloped, boyish figure, she is an idol to the 14- and 15-year old kids. She makes a virtue of all the terrible things of gawky, miserable adolescence."
9. Fashion editor Helene Gordon Lazareff says, "She looks pathetic. You say to yourself, 'Poor dear, I ought to take care of her.' "
10. Twiggy has twice appeared on the cover of Miss Lazareff's magazine.
11. Marshall McLuhan, the media expert, says, "Her power is incompleteness. Any person with a very undefined, casual, spontaneous image requires the viewer to complete it."
12. James W. Brady, publisher of a woman's daily magazine that discusses fashion, says of Twiggy: "She's not important. She's not significant. It's all a massive publicity stunt."
13. Mark Cohen, owner of a famous Boston fashion store, says, "I think she's the most obnoxious thing that ever came on the horizon. It's a pretty sad thing to say you're repulsed by a girl, but I am. Her legs remind me of two painted worms."
14. "Twiggy is completely disarming and charming," claims *Vogue* magazine's Diana Vreeland. "She's delicious looking. I love Twiggy and intend to use her in the future."
15. Harper's *Bazaar* editor Nancy White says, "I'm all for Twiggy. She's youth and freshness."
16. Hugh Hefner, owner-editor of *Playboy* magazine, says of Twiggy, "She's a refreshing change from the asexual zombies traditionally found in the pages of women's fashion magazines.
17. Twiggy is managed by Justin de Villeneuve.
18. His real name is Nigel Davies.
19. De Villeneuve "discovered" Twiggy in a beauty salon where he was a hairdresser.
20. De Villeneuve protects Twiggy and acts as her agent.
21. De Villeneuve got Twiggy's face before the public by bringing a portfolio of her pictures to the *London Daily Express,* thereby beginning at the top.
22. Twiggy earns one hundred twenty dollars per hour modeling in the United States.
23. It is predicted that Twiggy Enterprises, a company that manufactures clothing, will do ten million dollars' worth of business in a year.
24. A miniskirt in the Twiggy line sells for as high as thirty-five dollars in U.S. shops.

25. A whole Twiggy outfit will bring as much as one hundred dollars in fashionable shops.
26. It is not unusual for teenage girls in some well-to-do communities to pay seventy-five dollars for a Twiggy outfit.
27. A Twiggy blouse sells for $18.50 in some shops.

5 Organization

Support is one thing; organizing that support is quite another matter. You could have an excellent fund of specific details and still be frustrated about how to arrange them logically or to their best advantage. In the last chapter we touched upon an aspect of organization in our discussion of the paragraph on computer processing, yet we haven't really discussed outlining, which we feel is the best and most effective method for a student to organize his materials.

The sort of paragraph we've been concerned with so far doesn't require much preliminary arrangement. You've simply made the specifics relate to the controlling idea in some sort of sequence. But as we look forward to making the transition from the paragraph to the essay, you'll need to be aware of the basic structure common to both. It's our theory that if you can organize a first-rate paragraph, you can also organize a short essay. In fact, we think that many a solid student paragraph could possibly be expanded into a short essay, an opinion we'll try to support in the next chapter. What we're saying, then, is that if you can write a solid 150-word, factually supported paragraph that has unity, coherence, and good sentence structure, you can also write a short theme that has the same characteristics. That's the assumption of this book.

Outlining

In organizing a successful essay, you need first to outline the points you want to make and arrange them according to their importance. If you simply plunge in and try to handle too many ideas at the same time, you're likely to place small ideas where large ones belong and vice versa. But if you take time before you write to think about relationships between ideas, you can possibly save yourself some frustration and even some time. Actually, the outline can be likened to a tourist's guide, which aids you in arranging a rewarding trip. It gets you to the main points of interest without making excessive tours through the boondocks.

The proper form for an outline is indicated below. In our opinion, it's less confusing to place the thesis (or topic sentence, if you are making an outline for a single paragraph) and the conclusion *outside* the outline itself.

Thesis (or topic sentence): _____

    I. _____ Primary Support

        A. _____ Secondary

           1. _____ Tertiary

           2. _____

        B. _____

   II. _____ Primary

        A. _____ Secondary

        B. _____

           1. _____ Tertiary

           2. _____

        C. _____

           1. _____

              a. _____

              b. _____

           2. _____

  III. _____ Primary

        A. _____ Secondary

        B. _____

Conclusion: _____

The outline form is marked by various divisions, such as those shown above. The divisions labeled by Roman numerals provide the major or principal support for the thesis or topic sentence. The capital letter categories provide secondary support for each of the primary divisions. This secondary support is in turn developed by tertiary support, the Arabic numerals. One could continue this process of division still further, but unless you are writing a term paper or a complex essay, to divide further might create confusion.

The structure of the outline represents the proper positioning of smaller ideas in relation to the larger, more significant ones. The thesis or topic sentence contains the dominant idea—the large idea—and it is expressed in the form of a generalization. The primary support is also a generalization, but it is narrower and more focused than the thesis it supports. The secondary and tertiary support represents the specifics—the small ideas—that develop the larger thoughts. This last level is the nuts and bolts of the essay or paragraph. Thus, the outline demonstrates that old principle of subordination—proper thoughts in proper places—that we talked about earlier.

Classification

The outline also demonstrates the principle of classification, one of the most important concepts used in any kind of thinking process. *Classification* is the process by which large bodies of information are divided into smaller related groups on the basis of some principle of categorizing. We might demonstrate the concept of classification as it operates in an outline with the following example. Suppose the writer decided to do a paper on fighting men of the world. Perhaps one of his paragraphs would describe the typical Vietcong guerrilla and would attempt to prove that the VC operates efficiently despite some real handicaps. The writer might begin by jotting down a series of facts that he's accumulated through reading and research into the subject or even in actual warfare against the Vietcong:

1. The VC guerrilla can convert auto tires and old perfume bottles into military equipment.
2. He subsists on a diet of rice and sparse greens, whenever the latter are available.
3. He sometimes summarily executes the village leaders.
4. He has been known to make bombs out of bottles of gasoline.
5. He thinks nothing of walking over fifty miles a day.
6. He is willing to torture villagers, and women are no exception.
7. He weighs only about one hundred twenty pounds.
8. He can make a crude mortar out of a discarded washroom pipe or even out of bamboo stalks.
9. The VC guerrilla will carry one hundred pounds of equipment up steep jungle slopes for hours at a time.
10. He can live in underground tunnels for weeks at a time.

You'll probably see that the above list of facts, although interesting, hardly constitutes an organized body of information. The first task the writer has, then, is to organize and classify the facts—that is, divide them into appropriate categories.

In this instance, the various facts might best be organized into categories according to the characteristics they point to in the VC guerrilla. For example, sentences 1, 4, and 8 could be grouped as proof of the guerrilla's *ingenuity*. Sentences 2, 5, 9, and 10 point up his *toughness* or capacity to endure unpleasant conditions. Sentences 3 and 6 point up his *ruthlessness*. Sentence 7 would be difficult to fit into the writer's principle of classification, so it might be set aside. Perhaps it could be used later. The writer might now try a tentative outline, beginning with a topic sentence.

Topic Sentence: Despite the poor conditions of his situation, some of his qualities make the VC guerrilla one of the world's most efficient fighting men.

   I. He is ingenious.
      A. 1
      B. 4
      C. 8
  II. He is tough and enduring.
      A. 2
      B. 5
      C. 9
      D. 10
 III. He is ruthless.
      A. 3
      B. 6

Conclusion: Obviously, the VC succeeds in the sort of war he fights by making much out of little.

The writer might have more specifics concerning the VC guerrilla, of course, and they could also be included. But if they were too numerous, the writer might have to distribute them over two paragraphs in order to ensure against excessive paragraph length. In essay writing, there is no law against writing two paragraphs on one aspect of a topic, provided that aspect is important.

As can be seen, the writer has classified the traits of the VC guerrilla into three equally important categories. Then he has subordinated the specifics to their appropriate category. Failure to determine which are the major, or general, ideas and which are the minor, or factual, ideas can result in an outline like the following one, which fails to develop logically:

   I. He is ruthless.
      A. executes villagers
      B. will use torture

II. He can make a crude mortar out of discarded pipes.
   A. can make bombs out of bottles of gasoline
   B. can convert old tires into military equipment
III. He is tough.
   A. walks fifty miles a day
   B. lives underground weeks at a time

In the above outline, division II is not organized correctly. It is not properly coordinated with divisions I and III. It is a *specific fact,* whereas the other two primary categories are generalizations, as they should be. The statement which appears above as division II should therefore be placed in the category of secondary support. It illustrates the generalization that the VC guerrilla is inventive or ingenious.

A few additional hints about the setup and wording of outlines could prevent future errors. It is commonly agreed among teachers of writing that each category of an outline should have at least *two* divisions to ensure adequate development. Thus, if you have a Roman numeral one, you must have a Roman numeral two. If you have A under I, you must also include B. You may, of course, have *more* than two categories, but you should try for *at least* two.

Since the similar divisions of an outline are *coordinate* (equal), they should also be grammatically coordinate. Below is an example of an outline in which the writer has failed to provide division headings that are grammatically alike.

   I. Ingenuity
      A.
      B.
   II. Enduring and rough
      A.
      B.
   III. He is ruthless.
      A.
      B.

Obviously, the first category heading is simply an abstract noun, which is perfectly acceptable. But division II, which should then also be an abstract noun, is stated instead as two adjectives. Division III is expressed still differently, as a short sentence. All three should be *coordinate* and *parallel* in their grammatical structure. One possibility:

   I. The VC's ingenuity
   II. His endurance
   III. His ruthlessness

Another and perhaps better possibility:

Topic sentence: VC guerrilla is an effective soldier. Large idea
    I. He is ingenious. Medium
       A. converts old tires into military equipment Small
       B. makes bombs out of bottles of gasoline
   II. He is tough and enduring.
       A. walks over fifty miles a day
       B. lives underground for weeks
  III. He is ruthless.
       A. tortures villagers
       B. executes village leaders

Notice that the secondary supports are also grammatically coordinate and parallel in the above outline. The writer needn't follow the *exact* wording of the outline when he writes the essay itself, as long as he follows the direction taken by his outline. If the outline has unity and its categories are grammatically coordinate, those characteristics ought to be reflected in the structure of his writing. If the writer has taken the time in the outline to work out the relationship among ideas of varying degrees of importance, he will save himself valuable time in writing the final paragraph or essay. He will also be sure of a reasonable *singleness of purpose* in his writing. Another advantage of preparing an outline for your essay is that you can add to an outline if something important should occur to you after you begin to plan, and this will not necessitate rewriting the entire essay.

By this stage in your development as a planner and writer, you should be able to relax the rigid rule we made regarding the necessity for main clause unity. As long as each sentence (either in its independent or subordinate parts) contributes to the *point* of the paragraph, it could be said that singleness of purpose exists in the writing. You should also be able to make an outline of anything you intend to write. Outlining is the key to better organization, both in the paragraph and in the larger essay.

Summary

1. The outline represents a method of dividing or classifying a large body of facts into smaller related ones.
2. The outline should be divided into primary categories represented by Roman numerals and secondary categories represented by capital letters. Further division is also possible and sometimes required.
3. The topic sentence and the conclusion should appear *outside* the outline.
4. The topic sentence represents large ideas; primary support represents medium-sized ideas; and secondary and tertiary support represents small ideas.
5. Equal categories of the outline should be worded in a grammatically parallel way; they must be *coordinate* in the outline, although the writer needn't follow the exact wording of the outline when he writes the finished paper.

EXERCISE 36: *Ideally, an outline represents a descent from general to specific. In each of the following groups, the statements range from very general to specific. In the blank write the letters in the order of descent from the most general to the most specific.*

1. a. Last week a 32-year-old mechanic and mountain climber from Prague used an innovation of his own in rescuing three Frenchmen from the slopes of the Matterhorn.
   b. European mountaineers are a hardy and inventive breed.
   c. "Necessity," it has been said, "is the mother of invention."
   d. Adolph Zampach used a series of complex pulleys to hoist Jean Sembeau, Maurice LeBlanc, and the injured Gustave Bain from a ledge on the east wall of the Matterhorn.

Order of descent: _____

2. a. A 6-foot timber rattlesnake bit Frank Freeman on the right thumb, putting him in the hospital for a week.
   b. Snakes, especially venomous ones, need to be dealt with carefully.
   c. Frank Freeman learned about venomous snakes in a painful way.

Order of descent: _____

3. a. Most people procrastinate when it comes to Christmas shopping.
   b. Stu Rubine suffered a fractured left arm when he was knocked down an escalator by a 200-pound woman who was in a hurry to get home.
   c. On Christmas Eve, Stu Rubine found Macy's to be as dangerous as combat.

Order of descent: _____

4. a. Nothing ventured, nothing gained.
   b. To reach potential clients, salesman Frank Ginanni drives daily on Route 34, nicknamed "The Ambush" by local residents.
   c. In an average day, Frank Ginanni takes all kinds of risks to earn a living.

Order of descent: _____

5. a. While admiring a pretty pair of legs, Mel Milbaum stalled his rented Fiat on the Via Veneto, an event that led to a fist fight and getting arrested.
   b. When in Rome, do as the Romans do.
   c. For Melvin G. Milbaum, stalling his car on the Via Veneto led to the most embarrassing day of his life.

Order of descent: _____

6. a. *Anna Christie* played at the *Gay* last weekend.
   b. New Yorkers claim that any earthly thing a man wants can be found in New York.

c. In the New York theater alone, a person may enjoy a varied weekly fare.

Order of descent: _____

7. a. Philadelphia Superior Court Judge Elwood Webb today sentenced Emil Scopic to thirteen years in the state penitentiary.
   b. In recent years Superior Courts have been stiffening their attitude toward those who commit grand larceny.
   c. Cheaters never prosper.
   d. The court's sentence in embezzler Emil Scopic's case was unexpectedly severe.

Order of descent: _____

8. a. Bartley Maxwell's shares in several choice stocks rose dramatically last week.
   b. After being turned down on five successive occasions, Bartley Maxwell finally got a "yes" by revealing to his girl friend that his shares in United Tinfoil had gained fifteen points in last Tuesday's market.
   c. Nothing succeeds like success.

Order of descent: _____

9. a. In Athens, Monday, fiery Greek actress Maria Poppolopoulos gained a divorce from American actor Stuart Dixon on the grounds of his unconventional behavior.
   b. Maria charged Stu with listening every night to rock'n'roll records until she could no longer stand it.
   c. Greek "love goddess" Maria Poppolopoulos revealed recently that "American men are lousy husbands."

Order of descent: _____

10. a. Among Europeans, wine has a reputation for enhancing conversation.
    b. In a Budapest tavern, Tibor Laszlo did a lot of talking to the wrong person.
    c. In wine there is truth.
    d. Under the influence of a crisp Rhinewine, Soviet agent Tibor Laszlo made some significant revelations about an important dossier to a lady who turned out to be a British spy.

Order of descent: _____

EXERCISE 37:   *This exercise will give you practice in preparing a topic outline for a paragraph. Rearrange the following items according to their logical order in the form of a topic outline, just as*

*you would if you were outlining your own paragraph. The
topic sentence and the concluding sentence are included in
the details. Use your own paper to make your outline; des-
ignate the sentences by their number rather than by writing
each one out, as shown in the following example.*

Example

1. Upon opening its doors, one Washington junior college had twelve thousand students.
2. Enrollment is impressive.
3. U.S. junior colleges are a big concern and are getting bigger.
4. Administrative needs also reflect growth potential.
5. J.C.'s will require fifteen hundred new academic deans by the '80's.
6. "By the year 2000, " says one dean, "the J.C. will be one of the nation's largest industries."
7. Five billion dollars for J.C.'s in the next ten years.
8. In the next fifteen years, fourteen hundred new J.C. presidents needed.
9. Fifteen million dollars to be spent soon on one J.C. alone.
10. A million and a half students at present in U.S. junior colleges.
11. In five years, a million student increase seen.
12. Money allotted for J.C.'s is significant.

Topic sentence: 3
  I. 2
    A. 10
    B. 1
    C. 11
  II. 12
    A. 7
    B. 9
 III. 4
    A. 8
    B. 5
Conclusion: 6

1.   1. Hippies try new family system.
    2. Post office employs many hippies.
    3. A few hippies secretly subsidized by parents.
    4. Hippies eat a lot of rice and cereals.
    5. Hippie movement experiments with its own social norms.
    6. Family often resembles tribe.
    7. Says one San Francisco leader, "Let squares kill each other. We live, man, live!"
    8. Macrobiotic diet is hippie favorite.
    9. Sometimes twenty people live together as family.

2 10. Selling drugs earns some hippies' living.
3 11. Macrobiotic diet Buddhist in origin.
1 12. Hippies think of family as a "cooperative."
2 13. Hippies also have unusual means of support.
3 14. Hippies even advocate special diets.
2. 1 1. Migration of middle class to suburbs.
  1 2. Average-income people migrate to find space.
  2 3. Emphysema the nation's number 2 killer.
  2 4. Breathing Los Angeles air for one day equals smoking one pack cigarettes.
  3 5. Big city mayors have common problems.
  4 6. People with low incomes fighting for equal schools.
  4 7. Discontents of the poor and dispossessed.
  1 8. Two million middle-income whites have left cities.
  6 9. To solve city problems, United States will have to have dynamic mayors.
  4 10. Twenty-five thousand Chicago families on relief.
  2 11. Menace to health by air pollution.
  2 12. Highest incidence of lung cancer in cities.
  4 13. Deprived citizens strike for slum clearance.
  4 14. Minority groups riot during hot months.
3. 1 1. Party representation mainly middle class.
  3 2. Typical member afraid for job.
  3 3. Member earns about one hundred twenty-five dollars monthly.
  2 4. NPD (German National Democrats) motivation mainly fear.
  6 5. These signs worry Western observers.
  3 6. Member distrusts other nations' influence.
  3 7. Typical member lives in suburbs.
  1 8. Party objective is strong nationalism.
  3 9. Member desires return of Polish-held territory.
  1 10. They desire end of American domination.
  3 11. "The European Alliance threatens us," says one member.
  2 12. NPD man afraid for business.
  2 13. NPD voter commutes to work.
  1 14. Germany's NPD party extremely conservative in its characteristics.
4. 1 1. Wives expected to dress conservatively.
  1 2. Although dedicated, corporation execs' wives say that corporate life has its trials.
  2 3. Husbands must often travel excessively.
  2 4. "Whenever the office rings he has to go, even at 3 A.M.," says one wife.
  6 5. All these demands make wife's job trying.
  1 6. Corporation social life demands repressive conformity.
  1 7. Wives not encouraged to invite "outsiders" to parties.
  2 8. One exec logged 125,000 miles in nine months.
  1 9. Corporation women expected to drink, but only "one or two."
  2 10. One firm expects exec to put in at least two hours a day on weekends.

1 11. Some firms expect wives to entertain once a month.
2 12. Some execs spend three weeks on the road for each week at home.
2 13. Corporation men must place company first.
2 14. Wife reported she saw husband total of sixty days last year.
1 15. Wives expected to be "good listeners" but discreet.

EXERCISE 38: *Do exactly as you did in the preceding exercise.*

1. C 1. Despite people's valiant efforts, blob spread on Cornish beaches.
   1 2. Seamen on off-shore craft fought oil.
   2 3. Two thousand soldiers and marines scouring rocks along coast.
   2 4. Military fire-fighting units also hit rocks with high pressure hoses.
   T 5. Following *Torrey Canyon* wreck, English fought bitterly against oil spread.
   3 6. Women emptying boxes of detergents from piers.
   3 7. Thirty-six vessels working waters off Cornwall with detergents.
   1 8. Even civilians on beach battled oil blob.
   3 9. Smaller craft dumping tons of detergent in shallows.
   3 10. Army helicopters carrying detergents back and forth on beach.
   1 11. Little children trying to help with beach pails.
   2 12. Army and Marines, too, tried to stem oil flow.
2. 1 1. More than seventy thousand factory chimneys in city.
   2 2. Overcrowding major problem.
   2 3. Average dweller has only about seventy square feet of living space.
   2 4. Over eleven million people reside in city proper.
   3 5. About two hundred traffic injuries each day.
   3 6. Ten thousand new vehicles monthly in Tokyo.
   1 7. Policemen need occasional oxygen inhalation.
   1 8. Air pollution rate is alarming.
   T 9. Tokyo in '60's becoming urban nightmare.
   2 10. Fifty-four public housing apartments drew 400,000 applicants in 1966.
   3 11. Automobile increase brings problems too.
   1 12. Forty tons of soot fall yearly on every square mile.
   C 13. Except for miracle, Tokyo will scarcely be habitable in future decades.
   3 14. To purchase car resident must have off-street parking.
3. 1 1. Functioning as personal psychiatrist.
   C 2. Only superstars can survive without agent.
   1 3. Handling particulars for artists.
   1 4. Must keep client encouraged despite bad breaks.
   T 5. Show-biz agent performs indispensable services for client.
   3 6. Agents often handle legal details for clients.
   3 7. Agent sometimes "soft-pedals" bad publicity.
   3 8. Agent bargains with studio over salary.
   1 9. Planning publicity campaigns.

3 10. Agents even known to baby sit.

/ 11. Choose appropriate names for clients to better "image."

3 12. Agent must help client rationalize failure.

4. / 1. Many divorcees seek psychoanalysis.

/ 2. Some divorcees turn to liquor.

2 3. Other wives, formerly friends, distrust woman after she's divorced.

5 4. In several distinct ways, American divorcee pays for freedom.

6 5. Yet despite blow of divorce, most women readjust.

4 6. Raising children multiplies problems.

2 7. Acquaintances of couple often loyal to ex-husband reject woman.

4 8. Wife has less money for support of family.

3 9. Suicide rate of divorcees three times that of married women.

6 10. Facing psychological repercussions most difficult.

4 11. Children miss "male figure" in household.

2 12. Losing former friends inevitable.

4 13. Boys especially need father's help in doing things together.

5. 2 1. Fifteen-foot makeshift craft waterlogged, tangled in seaweed, half sunk.

5 2. On Bathurst, they found themselves in "green, wet hell."

5 3. Finally landed on deserted side of Bathurst Island.

2 4. Tropical cyclone blasted them off course far from final destination.

6 5. "If we had not had each other, we would have died," said Bourdens.

3 6. Tiny kelp crabs attacked their wounded legs.

T 7. French couple named Bourdens fought desperately in wild trial by survival.

3 8. "For days the big wind and great seas drove us."

/ 9. Lived on island rain water and sea snails.

1 10. Island jungle was practically inhospitable.

2 11. Heavy seas swept yacht five hundred miles off course across Timor Sea.

2 12. Raft trip attempted was even more hazardous than jungle.

4 13. Reptiles coiled together like worms in trees.

4 14. Crocodiles fought viciously within sight of couple.

C 15. Australian ship *Betty Jane* spotted raft four days off Bathurst and rescued couple.

3 16. The Bourdens' submerged legs began to ulcerate.

EXERCISE 39: *This exercise provides you with enough facts to compose a topic outline for a two-paragraph paper. Before planning the outline, answer the questions on page 112. These questions will help you in organizing your ideas for the outline. Use your own paper for this exercise.*

1. According to *Newsweek,* one Kennedy aide said, "If I was a woman, I'd be humiliated to think the public was reading things like this about me."*

*Quotations in this exercise are taken from *Newsweek* (December 26, 1966).

2. Senator Robert Kennedy voiced the family's personal distaste for the projected publication.

3. On the other hand, there are many who believe Manchester's book and methods are not objectionable and that he is committed by literary ethics to tell the bitter truth.

4. Regardless of the way the case finally was settled, it appears that in such a novel instance neither the rights of the individual to privacy nor the claims of history to truth will be completely satisfied.

5. "Bill probably would have done anything she wanted," said a friend of both Mrs. Kennedy and the author, "if Jackie had only written to him in a warm personal tone and explained that the way to honor the late President's memory was to make these changes."

6. "To the author and publishers this book will only be another transient chapter in their works: but my children and I will have to live with it for the rest of our lives," said JFK's widow.

7. The whole recent legal affair over William Manchester's book *The Death of a President* raises some significant questions about the public's right to know and the individual's right to privacy.

8. "No one else in public life has had her experience," said one man. "And it's being hashed and rehashed again and again."

9. The former Attorney-General said that author Manchester "had not fully lived up to the eleven-point memorandum of understanding he had signed."

10. "What a mess," RFK exclaimed to a friend.

11. Publishers Harper & Row and *Look* were convinced that the book was a major contribution, that "it was in good taste. . . ."

12. The author stated, "It has been said that I have broken faith with Mrs. Kennedy, that I took advantage of her confidence in me and that I recorded too truthfully her words and emotions. I do not believe this to be so."

13. Says one reputable historian, "You don't make contracts of this kind with writers. The idea that you can commission a thing of this kind is a kingly notion. It doesn't work in this society."

14. "I think it will stand on its own," said Manchester. "I wouldn't have taken a step in the publication of this book without the approval of Robert Kennedy speaking as a member of the Kennedy family."

15. Those forces opposed to the book felt that it constituted a breach of faith and an invasion of privacy.

16. Still other observers uphold Manchester's integrity and personal taste.

17. Mrs. Jacqueline Kennedy felt the book was distorted and prying.

18. Finally, the author himself believes he has acted in the interests of both history and privacy.

19. "To expose to the world at this time all [my] private grief, personal thoughts, and painful reactions . . . does not seem to me to be essential to any current historical record," said Mrs. Kennedy.

20. Many other observers felt that the work was extremely revealing and would cause profound pain.

21. Theodore H. White suggests that "A man who writes in public affairs should refuse to commit to anyone the right to review his copy."
22. Certain intellectuals, for instance, think that the pursuit of truth in public and historical matters takes precedence over personal privacy.

Questions

1. From the scrambled facts above, choose the sentence that you think is the closest to being all-inclusive, the one that could serve as a *thesis* for all the other details.
2. The sentence you selected in question 1 treats two aspects of the total subject. Divide the controlling idea of the sentence into two parts.
3. Now try to find two other sentences with facts that support the two parts of the thesis sentence.
4. Place these sentences in Roman numeral categories I and II in your topic outline. Your essay should be divided into pro and con categories.
5. Now try to account for the remaining sentences by placing them in their proper positions in the outline. Use only the numbers of sentences; don't write the sentences out completely.

Conclusion

After you have completed your topic outline, try reading each of the paragraphs aloud. If you have misplaced certain parts, reading aloud ought to reveal your error.

EXERCISE 40: *In this exercise you are asked to organize topic outlines that would be suitable for each of the following paragraphs, which are organized in a unified, logical way. In composing your outline, divide the paragraph into primary, secondary, and, if necessary, tertiary support. Keep the topic sentence and the conclusion separate from the categories of the outline. Use your own paper for this exercise.*

(1) The differing expectations of one generation and another might be dramatized in a discussion between grandfather and grandson over what traits distinguish an ideal college teacher. (2) On certain matters, there would be no argument. (3) Like his grandfather in the post-World War I classroom, the collegian of the sixties expects the teacher to have a sound familiarity with his subject matter. (4) And today's sophomore would probably also agree with Grandpa that the prof ought to be competent enough to publish at least a modicum of material in his field. (5) But while Grandfather would be willing to settle for that, his

grandson expects and demands a great deal more. (6) Today's professor should be dynamic, a man with the ability to electrify a class with a brilliant lecture at each meeting. (7) The teacher should also be fair in his grading practices and before assigning final grades should always consider whether or not the student is trying. (8) In addition, the modern student expects the professor to avoid indulging in a display of sarcasm at the expense of students in the classroom. (9) But the trait that today's student seems most to desire in his teacher is enthusiasm, and a prof will be forgiven a host of classroom sins if he displays that prized quality. (10) So while Grandpa appears to have accepted without much complaint the eccentricities and sometimes the tyrannies of his professors, his grandson insists that the student, too, has his rights.

(1) The college library houses an extensive selection of material for the study of art appreciation. (2) Art encyclopedias and large reference books are available in the library reading room. (3) Specifically, a complete art dictionary, *Dictionary of Art Terms* by William Netzley, along with specialized dictionaries such as *Abstract Painting and Modern Sculpture* are kept in the reading room. (4) Also available is the *Encyclopedia of World Art* by McGraw-Hill, which is the largest, most extensive art encyclopedia published. (5) The library also has a folio section where books containing reproductions of works by certain artists may be found. (6) The folio *Treasures of the Vatican,* for instance, contains outstanding works of art done in the Vatican around the sixteenth century by artists such as Michelangelo and Raphael. (7) Wendell Leon Nichols' authoritative *The Age of Titian* is another folio that has illustrations of most of the major art of the period. (8) In addition, there is a section for art periodicals containing information about the world of art, ranging from primitive art to today's pop art. (9) All this information is essential to a person seriously studying art appreciation.

(1) From the teacher's point of view, the ideal student blends together some rare characteristics. (2) He is eager. (3) That is, he needs little encouragement from the instructor to read 100-page assignments or write 10-page documented papers. (4) An eager scholar gladly accepts difficult lessons with the conviction that they will help to improve him as an individual as well as a student. (5) He is also disciplined. (6) On any evening, this serious student can accomplish three or four hours of outside study for each hour spent in class. (7) He can sit at his desk for long periods of time without the radio to entertain him or his friends to console him. (8) His most distinctive trait, however, is that he *likes* intellectual discourse. (9) He enjoys knocking ideas together to hear the sound made by the collision of, say, the views of Bertrand Russell and those of Pope Paul VI. (10) Such a person finds classroom discussion of Spinoza or Wagner or Shelley and their ideas as diverting as many other people find a good movie or jam session. (11) He *wants* to discuss the political concepts of the Kennedy administration or the economic theories of Lord Keynes, and he never feels that such speculation is a waste of time. (12) After all, the ideal student is an intellectual, a term

once applied by Marya Mannes to anyone who enjoys and appreciates the play of his mind for the sake of that play alone.

(1) Since the success of the tractor, farm machines have been developed to do an amazing variety of farm work. (2) Some machinery is designed for highly specialized operations. (3) For example, there are now hay choppers and hay crushers as well as hay balers. (4) And technology has also developed beet diggers as well as tomato-picking machines. (5) Huge "land-planes" for leveling the earth for irrigation are now commonplace in large agricultural areas, and one manufacturer is working on a machine for crushing rocks into a pulverized mixture that can then be spread back over the soil. (6) On the other hand, some machines now perform several functions. (7) The small, all-purpose combine is good for 125 different crops. (8) In addition, the forage harvester can be used for both corn and hay. (9) Finally, a few radically different tillage tools have appeared, notably the rotary tiller invented by the Swiss in 1911, a machine that in one fast and violent operation can completely prepare rough land for seeding. (10) It goes without saying that farming in the twentieth century is mechanized farming.

(1) In Sir Richard Burton, the adventurer, Victorian England produced one of the nineteenth century's most versatile men. (2) Burton was an explorer, for one thing. (3) In 1856, he fought fever and insects to become one of the first two Europeans to discover Africa's Lake Tanganyika. (4) During this trip, Burton also stumbled upon the source of the Congo River, a fact he realized only years later. (5) His stature as an explorer was matched by his reputation as one of England's finest anthropologists. (6) In his examination of the forbidden Moslem cities of Mecca and Medina, Burton reported with great objectivity on the mores and customs, including the institution of polygamy. (7) His travels into the remote cities of the Nile provided him with enough information on erotic rituals of the East to later write a best-selling sex-education manual entitled *Arabian Nights*. (8) To his other talents, Burton added an unparalleled mastery of languages. (9) In fact, he had at his command some thirty dialects from all over northern and central Africa. (10) These tongues ranged from Kanuri and Oji to Jolo. (11) Besides these, Burton spoke Egyptian fluently enough to delight the king of Egypt at an Alexandria ball. (12) In his spare time, Burton also mastered at least six European languages, including French and Italian. (13) Such multiple talents, of course, made Burton a giant among Victorians and also a biographer's dream.

6 The Form of the One-Paragraph Essay

To prepare ourselves for the expansion of the one-paragraph paper to a regular essay—let's say a five-paragraph paper—we need to take another look at the form of the one-paragraph paper. Perhaps it may be easier for us to visualize this form if we provide it with an actual, physical structure. The topic sentence, of course, begins the structure. This is so because, as we saw on page 1 in our book, the topic sentence contains the dominating idea of a paragraph. On page 1 we also saw that the dominating idea is a generalization and that the ideas that develop or explain it are specific, concrete statements. Another way of expressing the relationship between the generalization and the specific statements is to say that the dominating idea is the big idea, or the wide idea, and that the specific statements are smaller or narrower ideas. We can then illustrate the relationship between general-big-wide and specific-small-narrow by actually giving a paragraph a spatial shape.

We see that each of the three statements in the structure is actually smaller or narrower than the generalization or the big idea in the topic sentence—not because we have put them in that particular position, but because each of them focuses on one of the three specific and concrete (or small, narrow) aspects making up the one general statement or big idea of the boring Dr. Malcolm.

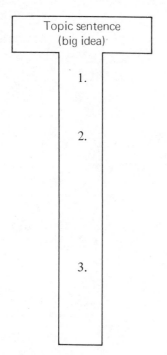

| Topic sentence (big idea) | A session in Dr. Malcolm's class is a boring experience. |

1.

1. In a voice as soothing as a lullaby, Professor Malcolm reads large chunks of factual information from the old black binder that houses his undergraduate notes.

2.

2. Sometime these notes must have gotten mixed up, because there doesn't seem to be any pattern or organization to them, which makes it impossible to follow his lecture. Malcolm's voice is not only soothing, it's so singsong and monotonous that everything he says sounds the same, whether he's talking about Fort Knox, the British pound, the gold standard, or the theories of Ricardo.

3.

3. But maybe worst of all is his habit of looking away from his notes (I guess he memorized them by heart fifty years ago) toward the far wall and then up to the ceiling, as if he were talking to God about Adam Smith and the gold standard.

Now if we look at the paragraph more critically—as you are learning to do— we see that, although its shape approximates a T-square, this is not quite the shape that we want. Something is lacking in our paper; the T-square shape is right as far as it goes, but it stops too suddenly and ends too abruptly. And that, of course, is exactly the trouble; it is chopped off, truncated much as you or I would be if our legs were cut off just above the ankles. Look at small idea number 3. You will immediately see that it is not an ending, a conclusion; it's merely one more small idea, and there is no good reason for stopping the paragraph at this point, other than that the writer simply ran out of gas. But that is not a good enough reason. Your paper should end only when you have provided sufficient support to validate the big idea, thereby satisfying the reader's curiosity and laying his doubts to rest. The end must always be accompanied by a signal to the reader that you think you have done these things and that you are now winding it up. Your conclusion rounds off the whole paragraph and completes its form. It is the last of the three basic parts—beginning, middle, and end.

Fortunately, most of us have an inborn sense of form, and at the very least we feel uneasy at a lack of form or at distortion of it. We want women's forms to be women's and men's to be men's from beginnings, through middles, to ends. We want books, stories, essays, jokes, and even one-paragraph papers to have form. We repeat, most forms have three parts: beginning, middle, and end. At any rate, if we pay attention to that nudge of uneasiness we feel when we see something unfinished or, for whatever reason, formless (shapeless), we are usually able to recognize formlessness, even in our own papers.

Now to return to old Dr. Malcolm. Since we already have expressed our controlling idea or big idea in our topic sentence about him, we have our *beginning*, and because we have expressed our small ideas in specific statements we have our *middle*, and the hardest work is over. What remains to be done—to add a conclusion or an *end*—is a relatively simple matter. All we must do now—and essentially this is how all conclusions are arrived at—is sum up, recapitulate the small ideas to recall the reader's attention to our big idea. We must echo the big idea, restate it, say simply in one way or another, "and now because of what I have shown you in my small ideas you can see the validity of my big idea—that is, how boring old Professor Malcolm's economics class is." Naturally, we are not going to say it in quite these words, but we will say something that adds up to that. Sir James Jeans ends his classic essay in which he tells us why the sky is blue with a brief summary of the body of his paper and the statement "that is why the sky is blue."

By now, perhaps, you are beginning to guess that if our paragraph with beginning and middle is shaped like a T, then a paragraph with beginning, middle and end will be a T crossed at the bottom as well as at the top (a double-crossed T)—or an I or the cross section of an I-beam, whichever you prefer.

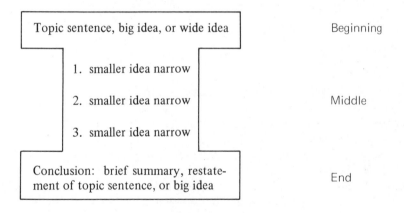

And now, to fill in the bottom cross piece. Since the paragraph is not very long, you could perhaps merely say:

Wow! Is old Professor Malcolm ever boring.

You might, however, wish to sum up the specific ideas with a more formal ending such as:

Certainly, Ricardo and Adam Smith would be bad enough by themselves, but with old Malcolm and his singsong voice, his old out-of-date facts, his humorless and incoherent delivery, topped off by his crummy eye contact [and now you restate your controlling idea] —well, if you want to commit suicide painfully, come into Dr. Malcolm's class and be bored to death.

Another variation might go something like this:

> So any way you look at it, there's no contact in this class. The students
> don't know what Professor Malcolm is talking about, and Professor
> Malcolm doesn't care that they don't know. To spend an hour at the
> mercy of a teacher who years ago stopped caring whether or not he got
> through to his students is my idea of the most boring experience in the
> world.

In this example, you might have noticed that we don't repeat any of the small
ideas in summing up the middle or body of the paragraph; yet observe that the
first two sentences in effect do sum up their thoughts; and often this is sufficient,
provided you repeat, in some manner, as the last sentence does, the big idea (controlling idea) of the topic sentence.

Again, a brief, indirect reference to the small ideas may suffice, as implied by
the "Wow!" above, which, with an ironic swish of its exclamation point, deftly
suggests all the small ideas and recalls them to the reader's mind. You might also
have noticed that "Wow!" serves as a bridge from the small ideas across to the
rest of the statement, which echoes the big idea. Often, a conclusion may briefly
summarize the small ideas and echo the big ideas without referring directly to
them:

> "Quit gripin', man," the voter advised. "That guy Doolin's a swinger."

Notice how deftly the word *swinger* includes all the detail (the small ideas) of
easy money, free trips abroad, beating legal raps. Notice further that in our
cynical society, *swinger* unmistakably suggests the charge of "taking advantage
of his political position for personal gains."

Deft, yes. We could do well to take as our motto for the composition of conclusions "the defter, the better." But not all of us can be deft—at least, not all the
time. Certainly, as compared with "Wow! Is old Professor Malcolm ever boring"
and "That guy Doolin's a swinger," our slower and stiffer *hence*'s, *therefore*'s,
so you see's, *so*'s, and *in short*'s seem stiff and stodgy. However, any ending that
does the job of recalling to the reader both our small ideas and our big idea so
that the reader knows beyond any doubt what we have been talking about will
usually suffice. We should remember that a simple ending, good enough for Sir
James Jeans, is probably good enough for us, most of the time: "that is why the
sky is blue." It's simple, and it works. It makes your conclusion dull only when
you haven't had anything to say in the first place.

We can see, then, that it doesn't make much difference how we organize our
conclusion, as long as we have one and as long as it accomplishes two jobs—
summarizing the small ideas and restating the big idea—both of which are an
unmistakable signal to the reader that the paragraph is ending. We can also
see that, aside from completing the meaning of the paragraph, the conclusion

is important in satisfying our esthetic sence, of which our sense of form is a part. What is shapeless or truncated (unfinished) offends us. What is complete and well formed pleases us, and a piece of writing has the power to please through its form as well as any physical object does. Hence, even in a one-paragraph paper—the shortest and relatively simplest essay one can write—we should never forget the importance of the form as well as of the meaning. If both meaning and form are present in a piece of writing, they blend into each other and become indistinguishable, as they should be. It is only for our purpose of studying what makes a piece of writing work that we separate the form from the meaning. Except for this, they work together, each heightening, each perfecting the other—if we let them.

To help us appreciate the importance of form in its relationship to meaning, let's turn once more to old Malcolm and put just the bare bones of the Malcolm ideas into our I-shaped paragraph. Notice that there are small ideas that follow each of the numbered ideas. What category of items in the outlines in Chapter 5 would these correspond to?

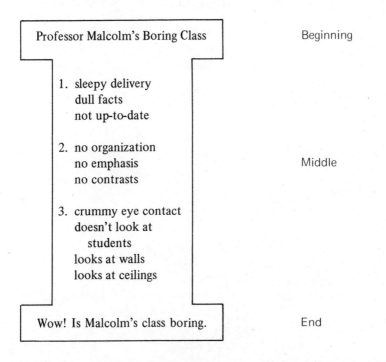

The advantage of placing, for practice, a paragraph inside a diagram is that it helps us visualize the difference in magnitude (size) of the various thoughts and parts of a paragraph or essay. Most of us need to see with our eyes in order to "see" with our minds. Hence, to have a diagram before our eyes helps us to place ideas in their appropriate relationship.

Summary: Form

1. The big idea or generalization or dominating idea—and big strong guys usually do dominate—is a part of your beginning or your introduction. It crosses the T at the top. It begins the form.
2. The small ideas or the specific, concrete statements that develop your big ideas make up the column or leg of the T or I. Often three of them are just about right. This makes up the middle part or body of the paragraph or essay.
3. The brief reference to your small ideas and the restating of your big idea— the summing up—widens your paper out again to make the bar that crosses the T at the bottom and completes the I. This is your ending or conclusion. It rounds off and completes your form.
4. Remember:

BEGINNING

Middle
Middle
Middle

END

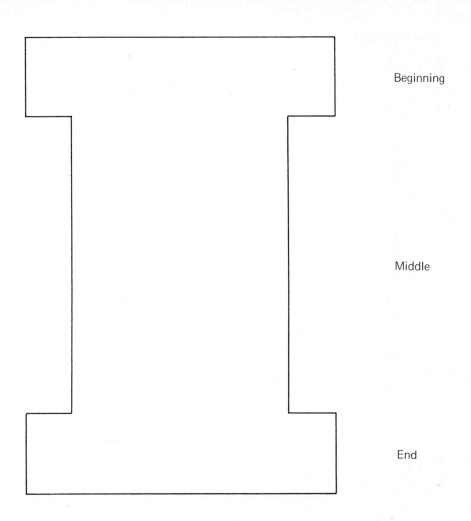

Beginning

Middle

End

EXERCISE 41:   *In the I-shaped space above, place in the appropriate corresponding positions the items from your topic outline of one of the paragraphs in Exercise 40, page 112.*

Undoubtedly, the resemblance between outlining and placing the topic ideas of a paragraph in an I-shaped figure had already occurred to you before you did this exercise. Now, of course, the resemblance is quite plain. However, seeing the topics inside a spatial shape may help you better understand the principles of outlining. Placing topics inside an I-shape might provide you with a substitute for outlining. Whatever you think about this, just remember that any kind of technique, device, or gimmick that you learn and use is worthwhile if it helps you to understand the relationship between form and meaning and thereby enables you to write better than you did before.

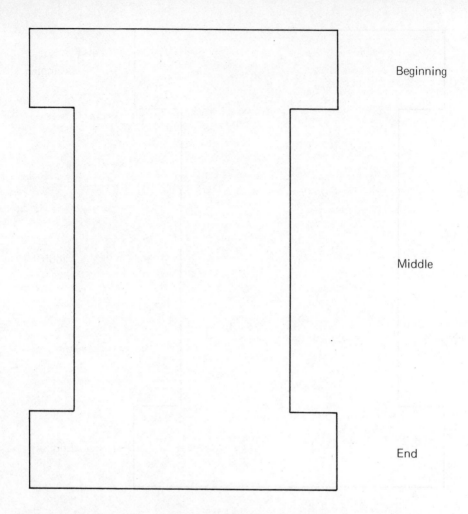

Beginning

Middle

End

EXERCISE 42: *In the I-shaped space above, write in the top crossbar the following topic sentence: "Each of old Olaf Torgerson's three children resembles him in some way." In the column (middle part) of the diagram write down a few brief ideas that show these resemblances and number them 1, 2, 3.*

Example: *1. Big Trygg has father's powerful but graceful build.*
              2. Peter has father's rocklike but thoughtful face.
              3. Little Looie has father's strong but sensitive hands.

Then, in the bottom crossbar write an outline of a conclusion.

Example: *By build, face, and hands, each shares something of old Olaf Torgerson.*
             Some part of the old man is reborn in each son.

You may, of course, make the children all boys or all girls or a mixture; give them any names you like; and of course take any tone you please—serious, humorous, or whatever.

EXERCISE 43: On your own paper, make and label a T-shaped diagram. Then write in the diagram a paragraph of about 150 words based on the Olaf Torgerson topic sentence. Make sure your paragraph has a beginning, middle, and end. Remember, for children you may substitute either girls or boys or make any other changes that might be more suitable for whatever you want to say about the Torgersons. A word of caution: form and the classification of ideas into big, little, or otherwise are not substitutes for thought. The awareness and use of form and organization will help you to think; they will not replace thinking. The variety of things you can say about old Olaf and his three children is almost infinite; but don't get too carried away. Remember the qualities in the offspring that you are tracing to their father must make some kind of sense, if not on a serious level, then at least on a humorous one. So don't forget to use your common sense.

7 The Form of the Essay

Now you are probably beginning to protest that not all one-paragraph papers are shaped like a T crossed at top and bottom or an I. You are right, of course. Some one-paragraph papers are shaped like an inverted T ($\perp$) with a bar at the bottom and none at the top. Others have nothing at top or bottom, but rather have a bar—or at least a bulge—somewhere in the middle ($+$). Some have no shape at all; but, as you have found out, they don't work very well, either. At any rate, these other forms can work just as well as our T-shape, but unless you are already an experienced writer, these other forms are much more difficult to use.

After all, it is logical that the topic sentence should come first. Remember, your big idea is not only the boss but it is also the guide. You look to it for direction. Everything that you say must follow the line of thought of the topic sentence. You cannot stray from the path of the subject of the big idea. Each of your small ideas develops the big idea by being about or related to it. Also, with your topic sentence as the first sentence of your paragraph, it is easy to check to see if such a relationship actually exists. For example, if the big idea in your topic sentence is the physical thrill of bodily contact in football, well, you must talk about that particular thrill, not about some other one. But since it is so easy and pleasant to let our thoughts stray, we might find ourselves three-fourths of the way through our paper putting down something like this: "and then I'll never forget the fun of just being part of the gang in that old football squad at Union High." By now if you have really tried to improve your writing, you have already found out that getting off the subject is easy to do. But you have also found out that with the topic sentence at the beginning all you have to do to see that you're on the right track is simply to lift up your eyes to that sentence, and there it is, as plain as day. Well, being one of the gang on the squad is fun all right, but it isn't closely enough related to the kind of thrill described in your main idea. So cut it out of the paragraph; it doesn't belong. There is nothing wrong with it as an idea—but not for a paragraph about the thrill of bodily contact in football. This thought brings us to another and quite different kind of advantage in getting the main idea down at the beginning.

As we swing into the activity of writing down our small ideas to develop our big idea, we often run into difficulty for three basic reasons: (1) we are not interested enough in our subject; (2) we don't have enough information to develop our subject; (3) other ideas related to but not subordinate to the big idea keep forcing their way into our paper.

The solution to the first problem, lack of sufficient interest, is obvious: change your topic to fit what comes into your head most easily—that is, what you are really interested in, whatever it is. If, instead of the thrill of bodily contact, you keep recalling the bus ride home late at night with all the guys singing and the annual banquet, then throw out the old topic and find a new one, the pleasures of being one of the gang.

In dealing with the second problem, lack of information, you have to be honest with yourself and admit that you didn't really have any right to choose that subject in the first place—simply because you didn't know enough about it. Instead, choose something that you have enough knowledge of to write about. But if you still hanker after your original big idea and have a hunch that it is a good one, that too can be taken care of by your going to the library and getting the information you need to back up and develop your big ideas.

The solution to the third problem is what this chapter is mainly about. First, however, we must clearly identify the problem. Often, an idea of equal importance to your big idea keeps cropping up, if not in your paper at least in your mind. You want to talk about both the fun of being part of the squad and the fun or satisfaction of achieving something either as an individual or as part of a team, whether in tennis, football, basketball, track, baseball, water polo, or whatever. Or maybe what had started out as a paper with its main topic the misery of playing second fiddle to a big brother has turned into a paper on the combined miseries of being caught in the middle between Big Brother and Little Sister with the old folks thrown in for good measure—the wealth of ideas and details depending on the depth and scope of your miseries. Then the more you look at these various kinds of gripes or miseries and really think about them, examples and incidents all supporting and illustrating these ideas begin to crowd into your head. Put them down, too, on your paper where you can see them, and keep going, listing all the things bugging you—Brother, Sister, Mom and Pop, car insurance, job, school, and the whole catastrophe. Then, if you are a serious student—that is, more interested in improving your writing than in proving your miseries—suddenly you will realize that your one-paragraph paper has become an impossibly crowded mess. So be it. Don't be alarmed. What has happened is that by attempting to develop your big idea through specific and concrete statements, by putting down many details and then looking at them, everything has conspired to make you turn out ideas. What you now have is enough material to expand your one paragraph into five paragraphs.

The main difference between the one- and the five-paragraph paper is one of scale. In an overall sense the form is the same. A five-paragraph paper stands in relation to a one-paragraph paper much as a heavyweight fighter stands in relation to a flyweight fighter: there is simply more to the big one.

Before we examine the mechanics of expansion, however, let's look at a student's one-paragraph paper that he later expands into a five-paragraph essay. Here is the paper in its original, one-paragraph form:

Although I agree that sports are important to students, I believe that the experiences a man has later in life are much more important to him than those of playing in the "big game."

Beginning

1. One of the greatest of all experiences of life after we are out of school is marriage. Here a young man is tested in ways and to a degree that he'll never encounter in a football game. If a young man and his wife are really in love with each other, they'll have a unity and teamwork superior to any football squad's in any league.

2. Many valuable experiences also occur when a man begins to earn a living. He soon learns the ups and downs of life as he enters into competition for tougher and for greater stakes than his competition in sports. If he made too many mistakes in a game, no one suffered very terribly, but now, if he is fired for making too many mistakes at his job, his whole family may suffer great privation.

3. Then in his declining years a man has the joy of not only his children but of his children's children and of growing old together with his wife.

Middle

So you see, the experiences of playing in the big game cannot compare in importance with the experiences a man has later on in his life.

End

Well, we don't necessarily see what the student writer wants us to see. Part of the trouble is that the subject of his paragraph is too big to be developed

127

convincingly in one paragraph or in a mere 190 words. His three small ideas in the column of the I, although smaller than his major idea, are still too large and too general, lacking the concrete specific detail that convinces us that the writer knows what he is talking about. The second sentence in item 2, for example, is more convincing than the first sentence in item 2, simply because it is more specific and because it develops the first statement. But there isn't enough of this kind of material to make the paragraph work, and even the "ups-and-downs" statement is too general and undeveloped; there simply isn't enough room in such a short paper to provide the necessary specific detail to develop so many general statements. Because the writer was getting his ideas down, he was lulled into thinking that he was writing convincingly. But he wasn't, he was only including generalizations instead of giving specific examples to illustrate the general statements.

The student, however, does have the fundamental makings of a good essay. He has the skeleton, an outline of his ideas that he can expand into a multi-paragraph paper. He has five basic items: the beginning, the three middle items, and the end—five things finite and definite enough for him to focus on. He can make the expansion without any desperate floundering if he keeps in mind the relationship between the flyweight and the heavyweight fighters and one- and five-paragraph papers. The following essay, representing the student's effort at expansion of the one-paragraph paper, is the student's reply to an essay entitled "In Defense of the Fullback," by sportswriter Dan Wakefield.

In Defense of Life

Beginning

1. I agree with Dan Wakefield in his standing up for sports in his essay "In Defense of the Fullback." However, I find myself opposed to his main idea that nothing we ever experience later on in life can compare in importance with our experiences in sports in school. The expression used in describing the so-called glory was the fullback's "eighty-yard run" in life. Accordingly, he is never again to do anything so great, and thus the rest of his life seems to be very dull. I feel that just the normal living of life contains many experiences far greater than that of the "eighty-yard run."

Middle

2. One of the greatest of all experiences of life after we graduate from school is marriage. Here a young man is tested in ways and to a degree that he'll never encounter in a football game. If a young man and his wife are really in love with each other, they'll have a unity and teamwork superior to any football squad's in any league. And the loyalty a young man owes his wife is based on a closer human relationship than the loyalty a boy owes the other members of a football team. Raising children is also a bundle of experiences of all types. Looking at them and knowing that they are yours and that you must take care of them and somehow raise them is a whole lot more challenging—and should be more satisfying— than

four years of looking at the other members of the team on the field and around the campus. Also, many men look at this time when their children are young and completely dependent on them for everything as the most cherished period of their lives. When Tad Jones (the old Yale coach quoted in the essay) made the statement that the "big game was the most important moment in a player's life," he must not have been thinking of the pride a father can feel when he sees his son graduate from high school or when he admires a portrait of his family. Certainly, experiences of family and marriage should be labeled at least as great as playing in the "big game."

Middle

3. Many valuable experiences also occur when a man begins to earn a living. He soon learns the "ups and downs" of life and begins to realize what competition really is when you're working for keeps instead of playing for fun. But this is part of the struggle of life, and the stakes are his sense of pride in his own worth and his devotion to his family's welfare. He learns the joy of doing a job well and being paid for it. As he progresses in his job, whether he's a scientist, an engineer, or a mechanic, he begins to experience the sense of his own value in the contribution that he makes to the world. Gradually he sees that his experience in sports was child's play in comparison with the events of his working career.

Middle

4. Another time when we experience so many wonderful things is in our declining years. Here we often become aware of the beauties of life. Perhaps the falling of early snow or the beauty of a spring day are very dear to an aging man. Often it is a strange experience for a man when he sees not only his own children but his children's children. There are so many experiences a man in his time of life can have. He may be living his life with his wife and growing old together with her.

End

5. Thinking then of the variety and the seriousness of the experiences of a mature man leading a life of marriage, work, and parenthood, you may agree with me that eighty-yard runs and playing in big games are insignificant child's play in comparison with the experiences of mature life.

You will see that the student has not been entirely successful in his expansion, but you will also see that it is a much better paper than the one-paragraph paper. Most important of all, you will see that the faults of the longer paper are not due to its expansion. That was pretty easy: the student used the same form and simply enlarged it and subdivided its ideas to discuss them in more depth and detail. Rather, the faults of the longer paper are still caused by the same sort of neglect and carelessness that accounted for the faults in the one-paragraph paper. But notice that, because of the clarity of form of the longer paper, no less than of the shorter paper (beginning, middle, end), the faults can easily be seen; we can isolate them and set to work eliminating them.

The errors and faults in the essay should be apparent to you, and you should be able to identify most of them. There are mechanical errors. The essay does not adhere to the principles of coherence and organization and subordination that we have already discussed. One of the paragraphs is better than the others. Throughout the essay the student fails to provide enough specific and concrete detail for the central idea. Nevertheless, there are some strengths in the essay— in addition to the enthusiasm of the writer for his ideas, which always helps make any idea interesting. In the main, the essay has unity, continuity, and emphasis— all deriving from its form. It is the form that provides the structure for both the original one-paragraph essay and the expanded five-paragraph paper. We are mainly concerned with form in this chapter.

Remember first of all that a longer, or five-paragraph, paper has essentially the same structure as a one-paragraph paper. Each has a beginning, a middle, and an end. Look at the essay on pages 128-29 and note the labels we have added. The first paragraph is the beginning; the second, third, and fourth paragraphs all belong to the middle or body of the paper; and the fifth paragraph is the end. To help you see this more clearly we'll put a skeleton of the five-paragraph paper into the familiar I-shape in which we first placed the student's one-paragraph paper. Thus, we have the following diagram:

Beginning	Introduction, thesis statement—paragraph 1	Big idea
	1. topic sentence of paragraph 2	Medium idea
	1. specific, concrete	Small idea
	2. specific, concrete	Small idea
	3. specific, concrete	Small idea
	conclusion	
	2. topic sentence of paragraph 3	Medium idea
	1. specific, concrete	Small idea
Middle	2. specific, concrete	Small idea
	3. specific, concrete	Small idea
	conclusion	
	3. topic sentence of paragraph 4	Medium idea
	1. specific, concrete	Small idea
	2. specific, concrete	Small idea
	3. specific, concrete	Small idea
	conclusion	
End	Conclusion—paragraph 5	

Now what we have done is put the opening paragraph in the crossbar at the top of the I. This first paragraph serves as the introduction to the paper, but at the same time it also contains the main idea of the whole paper, and because of this we call it the *thesis statement*—that is, the statement that represents the controlling idea of the entire paper. (Remember, the topic sentence in your one-paragraph papers was the controlling idea.)

Next, we put the student's second, third, and fourth paragraphs in the column of the I, the narrow part. These three paragraphs develop the paper's thesis just as the three small ideas in a one-paragraph paper develop its topic sentence, and in both cases they make up the middle part or body of the paper. Now keep in mind that each of these three middle paragraphs is shaped exactly the same as the entire paragraph of a one-paragraph paper. Also, remember that each one has a topic sentence with its main idea stated at the top or beginning of the paragraph. Additionally, each has three (more or less) small ideas, which we show on the diagram as "specific, concrete." (Actually, in the student's essay, every paragraph but one has its own conclusion at the bottom. Which one is it? How does it weaken the paragraph?)

There is, however, one very simple but important difference. The big idea in the topic sentence of each of these middle paragraphs is the big idea only in its own paragraph. It is not the biggest idea of the whole paper; it has now become subordinate to, or smaller than, the big idea in the thesis statement in the first or introductory paragraph. Because it is smaller than the thesis-statement big idea but larger than the smaller, supporting ideas in its own paragraph, we shall call it a *medium idea.* This should be clear to you if you study the diagram on page 130.

The small ideas in the one-paragraph paper have moved up to become the topic sentences (medium ideas) of the three middle paragraphs, while the big idea of the topic sentence of the one-paragraph paper has become the big idea or thesis statement of the whole paper. And this new form, the five-paragraph paper, is what we call the *one-three-nine* form.

One stands for the big idea in the thesis; *three* stands for the three medium ideas in the topic sentences of the three middle paragraphs; and *nine* stands for the total number of the specific and concrete, or small, ideas that we have in each of the three middle paragraphs. It might help us to understand the relations among these total thirteen (!) ideas and to grasp the significance of their various functions in contributing to the sense and form of the entire essay if we think of them as a family unit. Think of the *one* as a grandfather, of the *three* as his three sons, of the *nine* as the three sons of each of the first sons—grandsons of the old man. The first three sons are equal to each other and subordinate to, or smaller than, their father although directly related to him. The grandsons are all equal to each other and subordinate to, or smaller than, their respective fathers; although directly related to their fathers, they are only indirectly related to their grandfather. Keep in mind that of the thirteen, old Grandfather is boss; he was the original big idea, and without his existence, none of the other twelve would have come into being. A similar relationship exists among the big, the medium, and the small ideas in our five-paragraph paper.

131

To help you get a mental image of the overall shape of a five-paragraph paper as well as of the individual paragraphs within it, especially the middle ones, we will draw an outline of the five paragraphs inside the form of the entire essay.

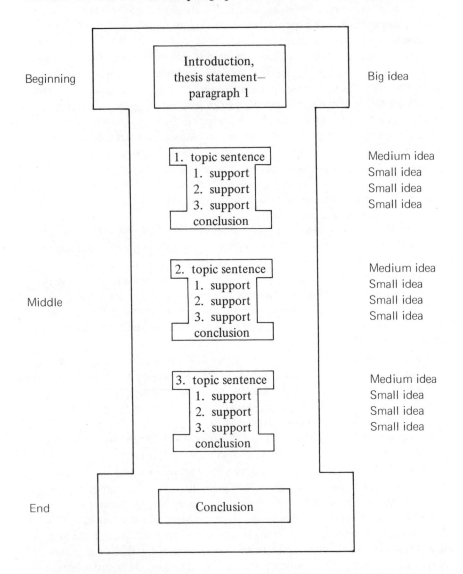

The next step is to examine the forms of the individual paragraphs in the student's essay. The first paragraph is diagramed on page 133.

Both the first and the last paragraphs are in the shapes of plain rectangles to suggest openness and a variety of possible shapes. We are not much concerned here with beginnings and endings for their own sakes. In the "beginning" paragraph, we recommend that your thesis statement be at the end with introductory

I agree with Dan Wakefield in his standing up for sports in his essay "In Defense of the Fullback." However, I find myself opposed to his main idea that nothing we ever experience later on in life can compare in importance with our experiences in sports in school. The expression used in describing the so-called glory was the fullback's "eighty-yard run" in life. Accordingly, he is never again to do anything so great, and thus the rest of his life seems to be very dull. I feel that just the normal living of life contains many experiences far greater than that of the "eighty-yard run."

Big idea
or thesis
statement

material preceding it. We prefer this for two reasons. First, you need some sort of background material to lead your reader up to the thesis statement—to show him how you got there, as in the above introductory paragraph. You need somehow to get him interested in what you are going to be writing about—anything to pull him away from whatever path of thought he was on to the path you want him on now, the path of your subject. Second, placed at the bottom of your opening paragraph, the thesis statement is followed by the topic sentence of your first middle paragraph, which begins the development of the thesis. Conclusions you are already familiar with. Writing a conclusion for a five-paragraph paper is essentially the same as doing it for a one-paragraph paper. In concluding the one-paragraph paper you sum up less important ideas contained in the body of the paragraph; in concluding the longer paper you sum up the medium ideas, which are expressed in the topic sentences of each of your middle paragraphs.

Because all of the middle paragraphs have the same shape and labels, we will diagram and discuss only the first middle paragraph of the student's paper. Remember that what we say about the first middle paragraph applies to all middle paragraphs in our system. A diagram of paragraph 2 from "In Defense of Life" appears on page 134.

Read paragraph 2 carefully. Notice how, by the simple act of diagraming the paragraph and by labeling its components, its faults and weaknesses are brought out into the open. You undoubtedly have many more ideas for improving this paragraph now than you did after reading it as it appeared in the essay. Is *marriage* the best word to use in the topic sentence? Should it, perhaps, be changed to *marriage and family life,* or *marriage and children*? Is the space devoted to the three small ideas uneven? Should the third small idea be lifted out of the Tad Jones sentence and be given more development and support by more specific illustrations of children's accomplishments? Or is the whole idea of children large enough to be made into a separate paragraph, distinct from the idea of marriage? Or, within the scope of the paragraph as written—except for enlarging further on the idea of children's accomplishment—is there a possibility of slightly altering the Tad Jones sentence and using it as a part of the concluding sentence (the summing up)?

133

One of the greatest of all experiences of life after we graduate from school is marriage.	BEGINNING Medium idea or topic sentence
Here a young man is tested in ways and to a degree that he'll never encounter in a football game. If a young man and his wife are really in love with each other, they'll have a unity and teamwork superior to any football squad's in any league. And the loyalty a young man owes his wife is based on a closer human relationship than the loyalty a boy owes the other members of a football team.	Small idea 1: love between husband and wife
Raising children is also a bundle of experiences of all types. Looking at them and knowing that they are yours and that you must take care of them and somehow raise them is a whole lot more challenging—and should be more satisfying—than four years of looking at the other members of the team on the field and around the campus. Also, many men look at this time when their children are young and completely dependent on them for everything as the most cherished period of their lives.	Small idea 2: joys of fatherhood MIDDLE
When Tad Jones (the old Yale coach quoted in the essay) made the statement that the "big game was the most important moment in a player's life," he must not have been thinking of the pride a father can feel when he sees his son graduate from high school or when he admires a portrait of his family.	Small idea 3: joys in children's accomplishments
Certainly, experiences of family and marriage should be labeled at least as great as playing in the "big game."	Conclusion END

"One-three-nine." It's a strong, tightly knit form, and we think there's no doubt that it will improve your writing. You have undoubtedly begun to wonder, however, if every essay must be exactly "one-three-nine" and why "one-three-nine" in the first place, anyway. In answer to your first question: Certainly not! An essay can have any number of paragraphs you feel it needs to make its point. It will have, however, only one thesis, just as your school has only one president. But the number of middle paragraphs may vary from essay to essay. A short essay (roughly any essay under 1,000 words) may have two, three, or four, maybe even five middle paragraphs, depending on the paper's length and complexity. Each of these middle paragraphs may have two or three or four or five or more small ideas supported by dozens of smaller ideas. In answer to the second question: we chose three and nine mainly because a 500- or 600-word paper usually requires about three medium ideas to support the thesis and three smaller ideas to support each medium idea. As a matter of fact, the number *three* turns up so often in so many quantitative and spatial, logical relations that many people have attributed to it religious, mystical, and even magical properties. We don't need to believe in magic, however, to see that usually three reasons, three examples, or three illustrations will provide more support than two—although often two will suffice. On the other hand, it is usually redundant or superfluous to cite more than three examples or illustrations to support a single unified idea. Three is usually just about right. Consider, however, the "one-three-nine" relationship as only a suggestion for the structure of your paper, and don't be afraid to vary the "three" and the "nine" to suit your needs in a given paper. The "one-three-nine" form is meant to give you a sense of proportion in the structure of your paper, not to strait-jacket you.

Summary: Form of the Multi-Paragraph Paper

1. The multi-paragraph paper is born when we discover that our main idea has several related but parallel and equal parts that can be sub-classified under one large topic.
2. Attempting to impose form on a smaller, one-paragraph, paper or trying to organize what are often at first only a few tentative ideas helps us structure the larger paper. This is so because in our search for form we begin to focus our minds on finite, specific concepts—something definite enough for our minds to "see" and begin thinking about. It is this process that releases a stream of thought with a sufficient quantity of ideas to make up a larger paper. This is what an old Anglo-Saxon poet writing in Old English called "unlocking the word hoard."
3. The multi-paragraph paper is an essay of about five paragraphs. The first paragraph is an introduction containing a thesis usually placed at or close to the end of the paragraph. The second, third, and fourth paragraphs make up the middle part or body of the essay. They develop the thesis. The main idea in each of the middle paragraphs is in the topic sentence, located at the be- ginning of the paragraph. Since these main ideas are smaller than the big idea controlling the entire paper yet larger than the *small* ideas beneath them, we call these ideas *medium* ideas. The fifth paragraph is the conclusion, in which we sum up the middle ideas and restate the thesis.
4. The overall shape of the five-paragraph paper is an I, the same shape as the one-paragraph paper. The three middle paragraphs also have this shape; they are simply smaller versions of it. The introductory and concluding paragraphs have a rectangular shape to suggest the relative *width* or the general nature of the ideas contained in them as compared with the width of those in the middle paragraph.
5. "One-three." That gives an arithmetical description of the one-paragraph paper. "One-three-nine." That describes the five-paragraph paper.

EXERCISE 44: *Analyze the middle paragraph outlined in the diagram on page 134 in light of the questions asked on page 133. Rewrite the paragraph, incorporating the suggestions below. Use your own paper for this exercise.*

1. Improve the wording of the big idea to make it correspond more closely to the paragraph's development.
2. Develop the second and third small ideas in more detail to give them emphasis equal to that given the first small idea.
3. Eliminate some of the generalizations in the development of the first small idea and replace them with more specific, concrete details for examples and illustrations.
4. Make the Tad Jones statement part of the conclusion and improve the existing concluding statement.

EXERCISE 45: *Diagram the third paragraph found on page 127 according to the one-three-nine form. After you have done this, study it carefully; then rewrite it, making whatever alterations are necessary to improve it.*

EXERCISE 46: *Using your one-paragraph paper on Olaf Torgerson (p. 122) as a base, expand it or some other version of the Olaf Torgerson story into a "one-three-nine" essay, containing about five hundred or six hundred words with five paragraphs— the introduction or beginning rectangle-shaped, the three middle paragraphs I-shaped, and the fifth and final (conclusion or ending) rectangle-shaped. Take your time and do the job well, frequently consulting the diagrams and explanations in Chapters 6 and 7, as well as the discussions of development in earlier chapters. This exercise will test what you have learned this semester about writing.*

EXERCISE 47: *Write a "one-three-nine" paper of at least six hundred words on the subject of life's satisfactions. This is partly the topic of the essay "In Defense of Life"; but we are not asking you to take that student's point of view or to defend any of his various arguments. Parts of his essay, it is true, may help to bring your own feelings and thoughts to the surface—either in disagreement or agreement—but your essay should discuss the aspects of life that you believe are the most worthwhile for you and that give you the greatest satisfaction. Remember the subject of a paper is not necessarily the same as the big idea; in fact, it almost never*

*is. Usually it is a larger, more general concept from which we
derive the thesis statement and big idea. As you can see from
the examples below, the thesis statement and the big idea are
distinct from, although related to, the subject. The thesis statement is more limited in scope than the subject of the paper; the
big idea represents the most important part of the thesis statement: it is the part that will be developed in the rest of the
paper. In example 1, the big idea is satisfactions from relations
with other people. The writer's job is to show in what ways
these relations are satisfying. In example 2, the big idea is the
writer's satisfying his curiosity about the future. The last sentence of this example is an example of a transitional sentence;
it suggests the direction that the rest of the paper is going to take.*

1. Example: *Subject*   Satisfactions in life.
   Thesis statement   "As for me, my main satisfaction in life
   comes from my relations with other people around me—at
   home, at school, and at work."
2. Example: *Subject*   Satisfactions in life.
   Thesis statement   "One of the main pleasures I get from life is
   the satisfying of my curiosity about the future—the future of
   myself, the futures of members of my family (or of friends),
   the future of the world. The unfolding of these futures is for
   me like watching a movie or reading a book."
3. Example: *Subject*   Satisfactions in life.
   Thesis statement   "My most satisfying experiences in life come
   to me from various forms of physical activity."

EXERCISE 48:   *Write a "one-three-nine" paper of about five hundred or six
hundred words describing the three main steps in a process such
as that of making a dress, tuning up an automobile engine,
building and installing a septic tank, getting good grades in
college, making a pair of sandals, or capturing a mate.*

EXERCISE 49:   *Make another visit to the Olaf Torgerson family and describe a
project the family has completed or an adventure they have
shared. Show how each of the three children makes his particular contribution to the experience from some inherent or
learned quality he has received from old Olaf.*